Physical Characteristics of the Bloodhound

(from the American Kennel Club breed standard)

D0119014

...d
rate
amount...

Back and Loin: Strong, the latter deep and slightly arched.

Weight: The mean average weight of adult dogs, in fair condition, is 90 pounds, and of adult bitches 80 pounds. Dogs attain the weight of 110 pounds, bitches 100 pounds. The greater weights are to be preferred, provided (as in the case of height) that quality and proportion are also combined.

Size: Height: The mean average height of adult dogs is 26 inches, and of adult bitches 24 inches. Dogs usually vary from 25 inches to 27 inches, and bitches from 23 inches to 25 inches; but, in either case, the greater height is to be preferred, provided that character and quality are also combined.

Color: The colors are black and tan, liver and tan, and red; the darker colors being sometimes interspersed with lighter or badger-colored hair, and sometimes flecked with white.

General Character: The Bloodhound possesses, in a most marked degree, every point and characteristic of those dogs which hunt together by scent (Sagaces). He is very powerful, and stands over more ground than is usual with hounds of other breeds. The skin is thin to the touch and extremely loose, this being more especially noticeable about the head and neck, where it hangs in deep folds.

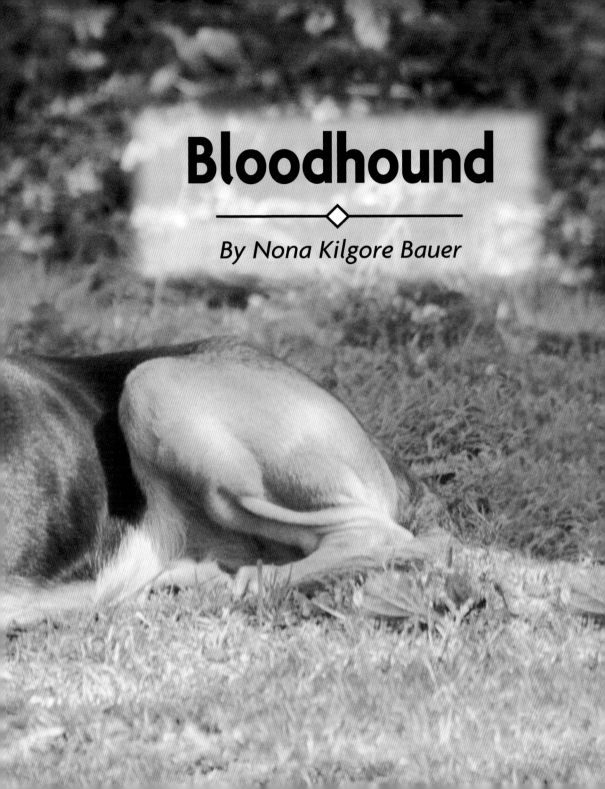

Bloodhound

◇

By Nona Kilgore Bauer

Contents

Healthcare of Your Bloodhound 99

By Lowell Ackerman DVM, DACVD
Become your dog's healthcare advocate and a well-educated canine keeper. Select a skilled and able veterinarian. Discuss pet insurance, vaccinations and infectious diseases, the neuter/spay decision and a sensible, effective plan for parasite control, including fleas, ticks and worms.

Your Senior Bloodhound 128

Know when to consider your Bloodhound a senior and what special needs he will have. Learn to recognize the signs of aging in terms of physical and behavioral traits and what your vet can do to optimize your dog's golden years. Consider some advice about saying goodbye to your beloved pet.

Showing Your Bloodhound 135

Step into the center ring and find out about the world of showing pure-bred dogs. Here's how to get started in AKC shows, how they are organized and what's required for your dog to become a champion. Take a leap into the realms of obedience trials, agility, earthdog events and tracking tests.

Behavior of Your Bloodhound 144

Analyze the canine mind to understand what makes your Bloodhound tick. The following potential problems are addressed: aggression (fear-biting, inter-canine and dominant), separation anxiety, sexual misconduct, chewing, digging, jumping up, barking and food-related problems.

KENNEL CLUB BOOKS® **BLOODHOUND**
ISBN 13: 978-1-59378-323-5

Copyright © 2004 • Kennel Club Books® • A Division of BowTie, Inc.
40 Broad Street, Freehold, New Jersey 07728 USA
Cover Design Patented: US 6,435,559 B2 • Printed in South Korea

All rights reserved. No part of this book may be reproduced in any form, by photostat, scanner, microfilm, xerography or any other means, or incorporated into any information retrieval system, electronic or mechanical, without the written permission of the copyright owner.

13 12 11 10 09   3 4 5 6 7 8 9 10

Photography by Carol Ann Johnson and Michael Trafford
with additional photographs by

T.J. Calhoun, Carolina Biological Supply, Isabelle Français, Bill Jonas,
Dr. Dennis Kunkel, Tam C. Nguyen, Pro. Dr. Robert L. Pfeifer, Jr., Phototake
and Alice van Kempen.

Illustrations by Renée Low and Patricia Peters.

The publisher wishes to thank Dawn Bather, Joyce Denwood, Gary Freeman,
Iain & Patricia Eason, the Gaillards, the Kretzners, Claudette R. Lyons, Celeste Meade,
Michael Moore, Jerrilyn D. Petty, Lisa Slinsky, Andrea & Dennis Teirney
and the rest of the owners of the dogs featured in this book.

This hunting pack of modern-day Bloodhounds from Great Britain speaks volumes about the history of this fascinating breed of scenthound.

HISTORY OF THE

BLOODHOUND

Few breeds of dog can claim the rich and colorful history that distinguishes the scenthounds from other members of the canine clan. In fact, of the many breeds of dog existing in this modern world, the hound is the most ancient. Dating back to the pre-Christian era over 4,000 years ago, hound development intertwines with that of man into a most important human/canine evolution.

The very name *hound*—or *Bloodhound*—conjures up impressive, vivid images: a massive animal with its nose to the ground, relentlessly tracking man or beast; a large and threatening dog in determined pursuit of some unseen quarry, whether victim or villain; a ferocious canine beast frothing to attack its prey.

The Bloodhound indeed may be its own combination of these romantic images. The name Bloodhound does not mean "bloodthirsty beast," as some believe the term implies. The name is derived from the term "blooded hound," which means a dog of pure breeding whose genes, or "blood," is untainted by other breeds of dog.

The Bloodhound as a specific breed was originally developed and bred centuries ago at the famed St. Hubert Monastery in the mountainous Ardennes region of France. The Bloodhound strain was then perpetu-ated by church clerics and those members of the nobility who fancied hunting and prized the hounds for their unique abilities.

Thanks to the monastic bent for keeping records through the ages, we have documentation of the hounds that are direct ancestors of the dog we know today as the Bloodhound. In fact, recorded history dating back to 4000 BC offers evidence of massive hound-type canines that were used as war dogs as well as hunting dogs.

The Greek historian Herodotus, born in the 5th century BC, in his account of the Graeco-Persian wars wrote of the dogs' great value during times of

From 1932, this photo shows Bloodhounds that were actual police dogs owned and used by the Chief Constable of Sussex (England).

both peace and war. Stone artwork from that era also substantiates historical data showing Bloodhound-type dogs with long tails curled over the back. Herodotus reported that the dogs were especially prized by the monarchs of Mesopotamia (known today as Iraq) and other regions of western Asia.

Another stone carving, dating back even further, to the 7th century BC, and found in the royal palace at Nineveh, the ancient capital of Assyria, depicts powerful hunting dogs who possessed the heavy heads and pendulous ears typical of the Bloodhound.

SCHWEISSHUNDEN

The black hounds of Ardennes were known as "schweisshunden"...slow, deliberate, heavy-skinned tracking dogs who trailed with great persistence and possessed exquisite noses and melodious voices. They originally cold-trailed game such as wolves, big cats or deer or trailed wounded game.

These dogs' importance to their culture extended far beyond the battlefield. Their scenting prowess and trailing abilities were essential to the food chain, since hunting for food provisions was as vital to survival as was victory in war. So it is understandable that such dogs were highly prized by royalty as well as commoners.

The migration of the hounds into western Europe in later centuries continues to be a matter of speculation. Historians theorize that warriors and migrants took their dogs with them as they migrated into France and England. The Romans described finding magnificent hounds with superb scenting ability when they arrived in Britain in 55 BC. These hounds pursued their quarry with a perseverance unmatched by any others they had seen.

Those same hounds were introduced to the French monastery by the crusaders returning from the east, crusaders who also brought other new kinds of animals, new ideas and philosophies. Named the St. Hubertus Branchen, after the monks at that monastery, these hounds were powerful, heavily built dogs, of medium height, who were somewhat long in body. They possessed excellent noses coupled with extraordinary hunting ability. Most were all black with red or fawn markings over their eyes and on their legs,

CANIS LUPUS

"Grandma, what big teeth you have!" The gray wolf, a familiar figure in fairy tales and legends, has had its reputation tarnished and its population pummeled over the centuries. Yet it is the descendants of this much-feared creature to which we open our homes and hearts. Our beloved dog, *Canis domesticus*, derives directly from the gray wolf, a highly social canine that lives in elaborately structured packs. In the wild, the gray wolf can range from 60 to 175 pounds, standing between 25 and 40 inches in height.

and occasional white marks on the chest. The hounds had superior cold-trailing ability and are the progenitors of all scenthounds known in history or existing now.

A few centuries later, when the Normans from Gaul (France) conquered England in 1066 AD, they brought many of their dogs with them. The St. Hubert's hound was among the conquerors' dogs. There also existed at that time a few white hounds, called Talbot Hounds (or Southern Hounds), large dogs that were also known for their courage and endurance. Talbots were another

From a 1934 issue of *Sport and General*, two Bloodhounds, named Eldwick Meuver and Malvo, in pursuit tracing a scent.

strain of hound that allegedly accompanied William the Conqueror to English soil in 1066. William and later his son, Rufus, maintained an extensive breeding program, breeding hounds that were used primarily for hunting

ST. HUBERT

St. Hubert is a small town in Belgium in the Province of Luxembourg in the heart of the Ardennes mountain range. The Abbey church contains the shrine of St. Hubert. The church and monastery were founded in the 7th century by Plectrude, wife of Pippin of Herstal. The spot where St. Hubert is alleged to have encountered a stag with a crucifix between its antlers is about 5 miles from the town.

deer, the favored sport of wealthy noblemen. Some canine historians believe that Talbots were the result of cross-breedings between the St. Hubert's hounds and other white hounds from France.

Never as popular as the black Branchen hound, the white Talbots were kept separate from the blacks, although it is known that in England some St. Hubert's specimens were crossbred with the Talbot. Talbots continued in France throughout the 18th century while slowly dying out as a result of public rebellion against Charles IX, who had bestowed favored status on that breed.

The St. Hubert Hound was held in such high regard in Europe that the English and French royalty and clerics often filled their kennels with large numbers of the black and tans, often giving them as gifts to high-ranking nobility. One record states that the Earl of Essex maintained a kennel of 800 of these hounds.

The hounds' impressive size and superb scenting ability pressed the breed into service in areas other than hunting for large game such as deer, elk and bear. Many were used as guard dogs to protect private and public property from criminals and violent crime. By the 16th century, Bloodhounds were used extensively to hunt man, particularly sheep thieves and poachers who stalked the Scottish borders. Their man-trailing ability was so valuable that the courts conferred legal status on the Bloodhound, allowing it to follow a trail anywhere, even directly into a private residence. Their testimony was so highly regarded that if a man refused a Bloodhound entrance to his home he was

FRANÇOIS HUBERT
The St. Hubert Branchen hounds were named after the monk François Hubert, who was later elevated to bishop and canonized after his death. Born to the nobility, François was an ardent hunter who maintained a large group of hunting hounds. After François's death, his breeding program was continued by the abbots who succeeded him.

assumed to be guilty or associated with the crime.

As happened with other breeds of dog, civilization and cultural changes affected society's need and uses for the Bloodhound, sending its popularity into a steep decline. The traditional large estates owned by the upper classes were broken up into smaller parcels of land and the surrounding forested areas became smaller, which caused a

A classic photograph by Fox depicting the high spirit and enthusiasm of the Bloodhound breed for the chase.

The scenthound breeds of Switzerland are close relations to the Bloodhound breed. This is the Bernese Hound, a tricolored hound known at home as the Berner Laufhund. The term "laufhund" means "walking dog."

decrease in the deer and other large-game population. Accordingly, hunters and wealthy sportsmen shifted their interests from hunting deer to hunting smaller and more available game like the fox, producing a need for smaller, faster hound dogs. Bloodhounds were crossed with a variety of breeds, creating the Foxhound, Harrier, Beagle and other similar breeds that credit their keen noses to their

dog show in 1859 proved to be salvation of these beleaguered members of the canine community.

That first dog show was held in Newcastle, England, offering an entry of 60 dogs, Pointers and Setters only. The next show, held later that year in Birmingham, was

Here is the Lucernese Hound, known in Switzerland as the Luzerner Laufhund. This breed bears a likeness to the American breed known as the Bluetick Coonhound, and is probably a progenitor of that hunting dog.

The Swiss Hound is known in its native land as the Schweizer Laufhund. As in all other Swiss scenthounds, there is a long and short-legged variety; the short-legged dogs are termed "niederlaufhund."

Bloodhound ancestors.

Breed population continued to decline through the mid-19th century. A few remaining Bloodhounds were still used in law enforcement, and a few others were kept in packs by gamekeepers. But the Bloodhound, along with several other breeds of dog, seemed almost destined for extinction. However, the introduction of the

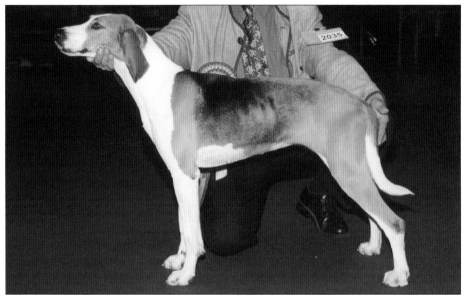

The long-lost Talbot hounds are believed to be descendants of the French scenthounds, such as this modern-day French Tricolor Hound, known in France as the Chien Français Tricolore.

also only for the sporting breeds. Finally, in 1860, the first all-breed show was held, also in Birmingham, and Bloodhounds

THE SWISS ST. HUBERT HOUND

Bearing the same name as the ancient St. Hubert's hound, the St. Hubert Jura Laufhund is counted among the nine scenthound breeds of Switzerland, known as *laufhunden* (dogs that walk beside the hunter). The St. Hubert Jura Laufhund, although a fraction of the size of the Bloodhound, standing 18 to 23 inches and weighing up to 44 pounds, does share the black/tan coloration as well as key physical features (heavy ears, loose skin and a large head).

were among the entries. The rise in the popularity of the dog show gave a logical boost to the popularity of many breeds, and the Bloodhound was no exception.

A secondary positive result was an improvement in breed temperament. Until that time, many specimens lacked an agreeable disposition, with some being either overly aggressive or excessively shy and nervous. Dog shows and the writing of formal breed standards impacted the breeders' goals and resulted in more companionable animals who were better suited for the show ring.

During that first decade of dog shows, Bloodhound success on the bench was dominated by lines

Circa 1933, Mrs. Russell Cook with Nereholm Falstaff, believed to be the largest Bloodhound in England. This dog would compete with today's dogs, were he still around to do so!

raised by two noteworthy gentlemen breeders, Baron Rothschild and Lord Haversham. The first Bloodhound bench champion of record, Druid, owned by Mr. T. A. Jennings, was from those fabled bloodlines. After achieving championship status, Druid, together with the Bloodhound called Welcome, was sold by Mr. Jennings to Prince Napoleon as breeding stock for the royal kennels.

All other prize-winning Bloodhounds during the late 1860s were also products of the Rothschild-Haversham breeding programs. These included the famous Bloodhound Regent, who was owned by Mr. Holford, and two other hounds, who were both coincidentally named Rufus. One

of these was owned by Mr. Edwin Brough, who authored, along with Dr. Sidney Turner, the first breed standard for the Bloodhound. Mr. Brough later wrote extensively on color in the Bloodhound, stating that although the most favored color seemed to be the black and tan, his personal preference was for the tawny mixed with black markings on the back.

In 1898 the Association of Bloodhound Breeders began to promote man-hunting trials as a sport. By this time, the only breed specimens available for competition were those who had been bred for dog shows and as companion animals. Yet those early trials showed that breeding for purposes other than hunting had not compromised the Bloodhound's scenting ability, as their noses proved to be as keen as ever.

At a man-hunting trial the hounds were required to run a

THE BISHOP BRANCIE

The name Branchen has been traced back to Bishop Brancie, a prelate who lived in the seventh century. Brancie was a renowned hunter who used such dogs on his hunting forays. One might further speculate that the Branchen may have arrived at the French monastery at the direction of Bishop Brancie, although there is no documentation to that effect.

simple line about a mile long, running the course in pursuit of a scent that had aged for about 15 minutes. Man-trailing proved to be extremely popular with the Bloodhound set, and the sport remains popular even today, with the ultimate prize currently the Brough Cup, a trophy named after Mr. Edwin Brough, the co-author of the first standard. Today's trail is much more difficult and is considered a prestigious event for Bloodhound aficionados.

During the same year that man-trailing was re-introduced, Bloodhounds worked in another, more unusual, capacity, serving as ambulance dogs for the Russian Army Red Cross in the Russo-Japanese War. A decade later, during World War I, they again worked with ambulance teams in Belgium.

World War II was another major turning point in the progress and development of not only Bloodhounds but also other breeds of pure-bred dog that suffered serious setbacks during the years from 1939 to 1945. By

Lt. Col. Richardson with two of his man-tracking Bloodhounds, circa 1930. Note that these working dogs are considerably slighter than our dogs today.

1944 the breed had reached a low point of only six registrations and faced near-extinction. Some breeders went to the Foxhound (who was created, after all, from Bloodhound crosses) to restore their lines. Only three English kennels, Brighton, Abingerwood and Barsheen, kept their stock free of such outcross breedings. The white markings that appear occasionally in today's Bloodhound may be a throwback to the Foxhound as well as to the white Talbot Hound that prevailed until the mid-18th century.

THE BLOODHOUND IN THE US
The Bloodhound first made its mark on the American dog world in 1888 at the prestigious Westminster Kennel Club benched show held in New York City.

HUNTER'S SAINT
St. Hubert is the patron saint of huntsmen. St. Hubert's Day is still celebrated in France, Belgium and Ireland on November 3. The feast day includes a special blessing of the hounds.

Like many of the
other scenthound
breeds of today,
the Foxhound
owes its keen
olfactory sense to
its Bloodhound
ancestors.

Like many of the other scenthound breeds of today, the Foxhound owes its keen olfactory sense to its Bloodhound ancestors.

Three Bloodhounds were exhibited, imported to the States by Mr. Brough. Mr. J. L. Winchell of Fairhaven, Vermont viewed the dogs at the show and was most impressed with their regal stature and noble bearing. He proposed a partnership with Mr. Brough and arranged for the import of a breeding pair named Belhus and Rosemary, who became the foundation of the first Bloodhound kennel in America.

Several other prominent breeders took notice of Mr. Winchell's move and imported Bloodhounds to add to their kennels and breeding stock. The breed was slow to grow, however, and by 1910 there were only about 200 breed members in the United States. At that time a hound imported from England cost upwards of $2,000—an enormous sum in those days—with some fanciers paying up to $5,000 for a status symbol Bloodhound. Over the years as the breed became more common, the price dropped to around $100 to $300, a more modest sum for a pure-bred dog.

THE GIFT OF HOUNDS

It has been written that every year for 700 years, the St. Hubert monastery sent three pairs of the black St. Hubert hounds to the reigning king of France. One of the kings, in turn, sent his own gifts of hounds to the first Queen Elizabeth.

CHARACTERISTICS OF THE
BLOODHOUND

ARE YOU READY FOR A BLOODHOUND?

Although the Bloodhound is a most remarkable animal, it is certainly not for everyone, especially the faint of heart. This is a very large dog that requires equally large amounts of space and food. The smaller of the sexes, females grow to be 80–100 pounds and stand 24–25 inches at the shoulder. The male is considerably larger and at full maturity can weigh 100–135 pounds and measure 25–29 inches at the shoulder.

Even the Bloodhound pup is not your typical puppy for very long. With a birth weight of 1–2 pounds, the pups grow rapidly, from 4–7 pounds a week, which is as much as many breeds grow in several weeks, and up to one-half to one inch in height per week. So while the Bloodhound puppy is a most irresistible creature, ungainly and incredibly appealing, he is not a "puppy" (in the normal sense of the word) for very long. He is best raised in a house with a large fenced area; apartments in the city are simply not suitable for a dog of such major proportions.

Bloodhounds have very expressive but solemn faces, characterized by heavy wrinkles and very pronounced flews and dewlaps (lips and throat). The eyes are not prominent; in fact,

If raised with children, Bloodhounds grow up to be dependable and trustworthy with them. Oftentimes, though, the dogs can be too exuberant for small children.

The Bloodhound has a very emotive face with heavy wrinkling that gives the breed a noble, profound expression.

charm, as well as to his uniqueness. He can sling saliva across the room with one shake of his enormous head, which is something Bloodhounds do adeptly and frequently. Many owners, in fact, find it convenient to keep "slobber" towels in strategic locations throughout the house. Moreover, this tendency to lavish slobbery wet kisses on his human friends may not be what everyone might call desirable!

Yet, despite their slobbery habits, the Bloodhound is a very clean animal. He is fairly easy to house-train if the owner uses patience and intelligence during the toilet-training process. He requires little in the way of bathing, and a monthly bath will keep most Bloodhounds clean enough to live with. Like most other breeds of dog, the Bloodhound sheds his coat twice a year.

The Bloodhound's temperament is, or should be, friendly, affectionate and protective. The agreeable factor, however, is somewhat compromised by his enormous size. The amiable Bloodhound who upends himself on both hind legs to lay his paws upon your shoulders to say "hello" can easily bowl over a child or a small or unprepared adult. Although he is generally very good with children if he is raised with them, his very size, exuberance and pushy nature make him an inappropriate

they may appear almost recessed or sunken, and the excessive wrinkling pulls at the lower eyelids, producing a sad and poignant look. Most are black and tan (the tan is sometimes called "liver"), tawny, or red and tan. The coat is thin, short and hard, typical of the hounds with St. Hubert ancestry. Their long ears hang low and are quite soft to the touch. The long pendulous ears are essential to the Bloodhound's work, acting as scent gatherers while dragging on the ground during a trailing exercise.

Those famous and most generous flews add yet another dimension to the Bloodhound's

companion for very young children. Despite his great love and devotion to the young members of his human family, he could unintentionally injure a small child during play or rowdy activity. Bloodhounds usually get on well with other dogs; thriving, in fact, if they are raised in an environment with other animals. Because they tend to be stubborn, or what some may define as "determined," and are inclined to pout when corrected, obedience training can be a challenge.

Of course, this same determination is an asset in the breed's best-known work of man-trailing. Bloodhounds are very aggressive when in pursuit or working on a trail, never giving up until they reach their quarry at the end of the trail.

In contrast to the many common misconceptions about the breed, a well-bred Bloodhound should not be aggressive toward people or other dogs. The ferocious bloodthirsty dogs that were portrayed in the famous American novel *Uncle Tom's Cabin* by Harriet Beecher Stowe, and in the subsequent movie of the same name, were actually mongrel-type cross-bred hounds with vicious temperaments that are not typical of the usually easygoing Bloodhound. To dispel yet another myth, those same mongrel

Happy and easygoing, like most other hounds, Bloodhounds are expressive and affectionate with their masters.

hounds were the kind of dog used in the early 1800s to track runaway slaves on Southern plantations in the States, a task never performed by a pure-bred Bloodhound. Those events, coupled with other printed accounts and urban legends, unfortunately perpetuated the myth of the Bloodhound as a dangerous and savage beast of pursuit. That simply is not true of this gentle giant breed.

THE MAN-TRAILING BLOODHOUND

Without a doubt, the most common and popular image of the Bloodhound is that of the huge hound sniffing his way through woods and fields to find lost children, escaped convicts or suspected criminals. While the ability to pick up and follow scent is highly instinctive, his unique physical characteristics also contribute to that special talent. His wide nostrils aid in picking up scent; his long, swinging ears scoop the scent up into his nostrils; the generous wrinkles crowning his head help to contain the scent. The loose skin also helps to prevent injury to his head when he is trailing over difficult or rugged terrain. Furthermore, the drooling saliva, which is such an annoyance in the house, creates a steam when combined with heavy breathing on the trail that enhances and raises the scent from the ground.

Beyond that, learning to trail a specific scent on command is a team effort that requires the training and education of both the dog and the handler. Beginning trailing should start in puppyhood, with games like hide-and-seek used as brief training sessions so the pup will not become bored or tired. The pup should be introduced early on to the harness and lead so he learns to associate the trailing work with the sight of the training harness. It is extremely important that any training program be consistent if the dog is to become proficient in this skill. The more carefully you

DELTA SOCIETY
The human/animal bond propels the work of the Delta Society, striving to improve the lives of people and animals. The Pet Partners Program proves that the lives of people and dogs are inextricably linked. The Pet Partners Program, a national registry, trains and screens volunteers for pet therapy in hospices, nursing homes, schools and rehabilitation centers. Dog-and-handler teams of Pet Partners volunteer in all 50 states, with nearly 7,000 teams making visits annually. About 900,000 patients, residents and students receive assistance each year. If you and your dog are interested in becoming Pet Partners, contact the Delta Society online at www.deltaso-ciety.org.

HEART-HEALTHY

In this modern age of ever-improving cardio-care, no doctor or scientist can dispute the advantages of owning a dog to lower a person's risk of heart disease. Studies have proven that petting a dog, walking a dog and grooming a dog all show positive results toward lowering a person's blood pressure. The simple routine of exercising your dog—going outside with the dog and walking, jogging or playing catch—is heart-healthy in and of itself. If you are normally less active than your physician thinks you should be, adopting a dog may be a smart option to improve your own quality of life as well as that of another creature.

prepare the dog and the better you learn to read the dog's reaction on a trail, the more successful you will be as a trailing team. There are any number of good books on teaching trailing for search and rescue, as well as organizations that offer camaraderie and advice on tracking trials and other breed activities.

The Bloodhound's man-trailing expertise is recognized in countless stories about man-trailing exploits that put hundreds

Although trailing a scent comes naturally to the Bloodhound, scent training must be introduced early on and be consistently instilled for success.

of criminals behind bars. So celebrated were their successes that many hounds of yore were shot by the criminals they had trailed.

The most famous of man-trailing Bloodhounds, Nick Carter, who was owned, trained and handled by Captain Volney G. Mullikin of Lexington, Kentucky, has been credited with over 650 finds that resulted in criminal convictions. At one time Nick Carter held the time record for successfully completing a trail that was over 100 hours old. In 1903 the Lexington *Herald* reported that in a single one-year period, Nick Carter had a 78% conviction rate with a record of 126 convictions.

Another pair of famous American Bloodhounds in the early 1900s were two hounds named X-Ray and Jo-Jo, both owned by Dr. J. B. Fulton of Nebraska. In 1902 *Century Magazine* reported that Fulton actually owned 13 trailing Bloodhounds who worked for law enforcement in a five-state area. However, X-Ray and Jo-Jo were his best and held the all-time record for following the longest

Though not known for their speed, Bloodhounds can be surprisingly animated and move with speed and alacrity. They are not designed to run for long periods of time, though they can chase down a potential foe when they have to.

THE AGE OF ROBO-DOG

Studies at the Center for the Human-Animal Bond show that children who interact with pets benefit physiologically, socially and educationally. Dogs, in particular, increase children's learning capacities and expand their abilities to function in social situations. Families with young children commonly add a canine to their homes.

Enter Robo-dog. Efforts to create a robotic canine companion are fast underway, and there have been some interesting results. It is the hope of scientists that the interaction between robotic dogs and children will shed light on the physical, mental, moral and social concepts of such relationships. Robotic dogs offer many advantages over real dogs—they don't require food or water and never have accidents indoors. Even so, Robo-dogs will never take the place of real dogs—even George Jetson's futuristic family included Astro, a real-live dog! It is curious that 21st-century humans would invest so much money and energy into inventing robots to do for us what dogs have been doing for centuries for nothing more than a pat on the head and a bowl of food.

element. Many Bloodhound owners who raised and trained man-trailers were frequently called upon to locate missing children. Modern law enforcement in Britain, the United States and other countries still make use of the famous Bloodhound nose despite all of the modern technology involved in the pursuit of criminals. Professionalism in the training and handling of Bloodhounds has given rise to Bloodhound associations in many countries, on several continents, that are affiliated with local police agencies. With their primary goal of training Bloodhounds by time-tested and proven methods, many associations hold seminars to assist in the training and handling of the hounds, as well as offering technical advice from acknowledged experts in the field of man-trailing.

HEREDITARY DISEASE AND HEALTH CONCERNS

Every breed of pure-bred dog faces the challenge of hereditary diseases that threaten its health. Responsible breeders are knowledgeable about the conditions that can be passed on genetically from the dam and sire to the litter, and therefore screen breeding stock before planning a mating. The following hereditary concerns are provided to make the potential owner aware of the problems that face Bloodhounds

trail, 135 miles across the state of Kansas, leading the police to the criminal for whom they were hunting.

Not all famous man-trailing exploits pursued the criminal

DO YOU KNOW ABOUT HIP DYSPLASIA?

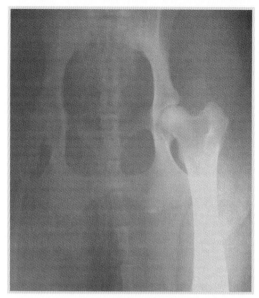

X-ray of a dog with "Good" hips.

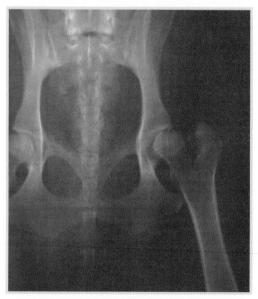

X-ray of a dog with "Moderate" dysplastic hips.

Hip dysplasia is a fairly common condition found in pure-bred dogs. When a dog has hip dysplasia, his hind leg has an incorrectly formed hip joint. By constant use of the hip joint, it becomes more and more loose, wears abnormally and may become arthritic.

Hip dysplasia can only be confirmed with an x-ray, but certain symptoms may indicate a problem. Your dog may have a hip dysplasia problem if he walks in a peculiar manner, hops instead of smoothly runs, uses his hind legs in unison (to keep the pressure off the weak joint), has trouble getting up from a prone position or always sits with both legs together on one side of his body.

As the dog matures, he may adapt well to life with a bad hip, but in a few years the arthritis develops and many dogs with hip dysplasia become crippled.

Hip dysplasia is considered an inherited disease and only can be diagnosed definitively by x-ray when the dog is two years old, although symptoms often appear earlier. Some experts claim that a special diet might help your puppy outgrow the bad hip, but the usual treatments are surgical. The removal of the pectineus muscle, the removal of the round part of the femur, reconstructing the pelvis and replacing the hip with an artificial one are all surgical interventions that are expensive, but they are usually very successful. Follow the advice of your veterinarian.

in the 21st century. Discuss all of them with your chosen breeder and feel confident that your puppy will not be facing difficulties due to irresponsible breeding, failure to screen stock or lack of knowledge.

Hip Dysplasia (HD)

Like most other working breeds, Bloodhounds are prone to hip dysplasia, which is a potentially crippling disease that affects the hip joints. It is caused by poor bone formation of the femur (upper leg bone) where it fits into the socket of the hip. Hip dysplasia can be very painful and usually causes arthritis in later years. The condition is thought to be inherited through a complex combination of genetic and environmental factors, and a wise puppy buyer should look for good hips in several generations of a pedigree before purchasing a puppy.

Hip dysplasia is diagnosed by x-ray, with cleared hips receiving a clearance certificate from the British Veterinary Association and the American Kennel Club. In the United States, the clearing house for hips is the Orthopedic Foundation for Animals (OFA). All responsible breeders screen their breeding stock for hip dysplasia and obtain the necessary certificates of clearance before breeding any dog.

Current research into the

DOGS, DOGS, GOOD FOR YOUR HEART!
People usually purchase dogs for companionship, but studies show that dogs can help to improve their owners' health and level of activity, as well as lower a human's risk of coronary heart disease. Without even realizing it, when a person puts time into exercising, grooming and feeding a dog, he also puts more time into his own personal health care. Dog owners establish more routine schedules for their dogs to follow, which can have positive effects on their own health. Dogs also teach us patience, offer unconditional love and provide the joy of having a furry friend to pet!

Lower entropion, or rolling in of the eyelid, is causing irritation in the left eye of a young dog. Several extra eyelashes, or distichiasis, are present on the upper lid. Photo courtesy of Prof. Dr. Robert L. Peifer, Jr.

cause(s) and control of hip dysplasia indicates that overfeeding and feeding a diet high in calories (primarily fat) during a large-breed puppy's rapid-growth stages may contribute to the onset of HD. Heavy-bodied and overweight puppies are more at risk than

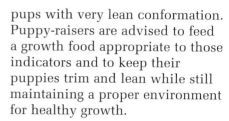

pups with very lean conformation. Puppy-raisers are advised to feed a growth food appropriate to those indicators and to keep their puppies trim and lean while still maintaining a proper environment for healthy growth.

ENTROPION

Given their heavily wrinkled brows, it comes as no surprise that Bloodhounds can be prone to entropion, a condition where the eyelid rolls inward, causing the eyelashes to rub the cornea, which is quite painful to the dog. Eventual scarring may cause some vision loss. It can be corrected surgically, but affected dogs may pass that gene along to their offspring and should not be bred.

GASTRIC DILATATION-VOLVULUS (GDV)/BLOAT

Gastric dilatation-volvulus, also known as gastric torsion, and more commonly as bloat, is a condition that primarily affects deep-chested breeds of dog. For reasons still unknown to veterinary science, the stomach of the animal suddenly fills with gas and begins to twist, cutting off the blood supply and causing shock and death within a matter of hours. Immediate veterinary care is imperative if the dog is to survive. Because of their physical structure, Bloodhounds are very prone to bloat. The risk can be minimized by feeding several

ELEVATED BOWLS

Feeding your dog from elevated bowls has been long thought to be an effective bloat preventative, but new research suggests that may not be the case. Some owners feed their dogs from elevated bowls to prevent their eating too rapidly, but it is sometimes now advised not to feed from elevated bowls if dealing with a bloat-prone breed. Unfortunately, there is no surefire way to prevent bloat, and even the causes are not known for sure. Use common sense and know your dog so that you can recognize the signs when his health is compromised and get to the vet right away.

BLOAT-PREVENTION TIPS

As varied as the causes of bloat are the tips for prevention, and some common preventative methods follow:

- Feed two or three small meals daily rather than one large one;
- Do not feed water before, after or with meals, but allow access to water at all other times;
- Never permit rapid eating or gulping of water;
- No exercise for the dog at least two hours before and (especially) after meals;
- Feed high-quality food with adequate protein, adequate fiber content and not too much fat and carbohydrate;
- Explore herbal additives, enzymes or gas-reduction products (only under a vet's advice) to encourage a "friendly" environment in the dog's digestive system;
- Avoid foods and ingredients known to produce gas;
- Avoid stressful situations for the dog, especially at mealtimes;
- Make dietary changes gradually, over a period of a few weeks;
- Do not feed dry food only;
- Although the role of genetics is not known, many breeders do not breed from previously affected dogs;
- Sometimes owners are advised to have gastroplexy (stomach stapling) performed on their dogs as a preventative measure;
- Pay attention to your dog's behavior and any changes that could be symptomatic of bloat. Your dog's life depends on it!

small meals instead of one or two very large meals, and limiting exercise before and after eating, with "minimize" being the key word in prevention. Every Bloodhound owner should familiarize himself with the physical symptoms of bloat and proper emergency care in the sad event that the dog falls victim to this life-threatening condition.

ALLERGIES

Allergies are common in the Bloodhound, showing up as sensitivities to environmental factors such as pollens, various mites, and/or food products. A good general reference on the different types of allergies and how to treat them is recommended for Bloodhound owners.

For deep-chested dogs that are prone to bloat, an elevated bowl stand is sometimes recommended to keep the Bloodhound from craning his neck while eating.

At a dog show, the Bloodhound that the judge deems closest to the breed standard is the winner. It is understood that no dog can ever possess every specific point that the standard defines.

BREED STANDARD FOR THE

BLOODHOUND

Every breed that is recognized by one of the national or international breed registries is guided by a "standard," a detailed description of the dog's physical appearance, its temperament and its natural ability. Breed standards are obviously extremely important to the future of any breed, as without specific guidelines, breeders could alter or completely lose or eliminate the very nature of a breed within just a few generations. Because breeders recognize that it is impossible to produce a perfect dog of any breed, responsible individuals can only do their best to select and breed the best representatives of their chosen breed. Most good breeders also have a general knowledge of genetics and understand the role that dominant and recessive genes play when they plan a litter of pups.

Judges, like breeders, use the standard to make important decisions. It is the breed standard that forms the judge's "mind's eye" when he is evaluating dogs in the show ring. The judge's choice, the winner of a class, is the dog that most closely conforms to the dog depicted in the breed standard. The notion of a conformation show is to select the dog that "conforms" most closely to the standard.

AMERICAN KENNEL CLUB STANDARD FOR THE BLOODHOUND

General Character: The Bloodhound possesses, in a most marked degree, every point and

Standing for the judge's inspection, this Bloodhound possesses many of the desired features that the standard enumerates, though the judge's opinion will be the one that counts on the day of the show.

characteristic of those dogs which hunt together by scent (Sagaces). He is very powerful, and stands over more ground than is usual with hounds of other breeds. The skin is thin to the touch and

The head should be narrow in proportion to length, and long in proportion to body.

extremely loose, this being more especially noticeable about the head and neck, where it hangs in deep folds.

Height: The mean average height of adult dogs is 26 inches, and of adult bitches 24 inches. Dogs usually vary from 25 inches to 27 inches, and bitches from 23 inches to 25 inches; but, in either case, the greater height is to be preferred, provided that character and quality are also combined.

Weight: The mean average weight of adult dogs, in fair condition, is 90 pounds, and of adult bitches 80 pounds. Dogs attain the weight of 110 pounds, bitches 100 pounds. The greater weights are to be preferred, provided (as in the case of height) that quality and proportion are also combined.

Expression: The expression is noble and dignified, and characterized by solemnity, wisdom, and power.

Temperament: In temperament he is extremely affectionate, neither quarrelsome with companions nor with other dogs. His nature is somewhat shy, and equally sensitive to kindness or correction by his master.

Head: The head is narrow in proportion to its length, and long in proportion to the body,

tapering but slightly from the temples to the end of the muzzle, thus (when viewed from above and in front) having the appearance of being flattened at the sides and of being nearly equal in width throughout its entire length. In profile the upper outline of the skull is nearly in the same plane as that of the foreface. The length from end of nose to stop (midway between the eyes) should be not less than that from stop to back of occipital protuberance (peak). The entire length of head from the posterior part of the occipital protuberance to the end of the muzzle should be 12 inches, or more, in dogs, and 11 inches, or more, in bitches. *Skull*—The skull is long and narrow, with the occipital peak very pronounced. The brows are not prominent, although, owing to the deep-set eyes, they may have that appearance. *Foreface*—The foreface is long, deep, and of even width throughout, with square outline when seen in profile. *Eyes*—The eyes are deeply sunk in the orbits, the lids assuming a lozenge or diamond shape, in consequence of the lower lids being dragged down and everted by the heavy flews. The eyes correspond with the general tone of color of the animal, varying from deep hazel to yellow. The hazel color is, however, to be preferred, although very seldom seen in liver-and-tan hounds. *Ears*—The ears are thin and soft to the touch, extremely long, set very low, and fall in graceful folds, the lower parts curling inward and backward. *Mouth*—A scissors bite is preferred, level bite accepted.

Wrinkle: The head is furnished with an amount of loose skin, which in nearly every position appears superabundant, but more particularly so when the head is carried low; the skin then falls into loose, pendulous ridges and folds, especially over the forehead and sides of the face. *Nostrils*—The nostrils are large and open. *Lips, Flews, and Dewlap*—In front the lips fall squarely, making a right angle with the upper line of the foreface; while behind they form deep, hanging flews, and, being continued into the pendant folds of loose skin about the neck, constitute the dewlap, which is very pronounced. These charac-teristics are found, though in a

lesser degree, in the bitch.

Neck, Shoulders and Chest: The neck is long, the shoulders muscular and well sloped backwards; the ribs are well sprung; and the chest well let down between the forelegs, forming a deep keel.

Legs and Feet: The forelegs are straight and large in bone, with elbows squarely set; the feet strong and well knuckled up; the thighs and second thighs (gaskins) are very muscular; the hocks well bent and let down and squarely set.

Back and Loin: The back and loins are strong, the latter deep and slightly arched. *Stern*—The stern is long and tapering, and set on rather high, with a moderate amount of hair underneath.

Gait: The gait is elastic, swinging and free, the stern being carried high, but not too much curled over the back.

Bitches rarely do as well as dogs in the show ring, though this lovely Bloodhound bitch has much to offer. From her sweet expression to the tip of her long, tapering tail, she is a lovely specimen.

Color: The colors are black and tan, liver and tan, and red; the darker colors being sometimes interspersed with lighter or badger-colored hair, and sometimes flecked with white. A small amount of white is permissible on chest, feet, and tip of stern.

Approved: January 9, 1996
Effective: February 29, 1996

AUTHOR'S ANNOTATIONS
"Standing over more ground than other hounds" may be a bit confusing to the novice. This passage refers (at the time the standard was drawn up) to the smaller, more fashionable hounds of that time, Foxhounds, Harriers and Beagles, all of whom are shorter-coupled dogs.

Bloodhounds of the past have been known to be quite aggressive, a quality that today is severely faulted, even moreso than the dog who is overtly shy.

In some cases, the weight of the extra loose skin can cause the lower eyelid to hang lower yet and turn outward, causing some of the eye problems typical in the breed. The descriptions of the nostrils, skin and dewlaps are of particular importance since they directly affect the Bloodhound's ability to trail.

"Low ear set" means just below the level of the eye.

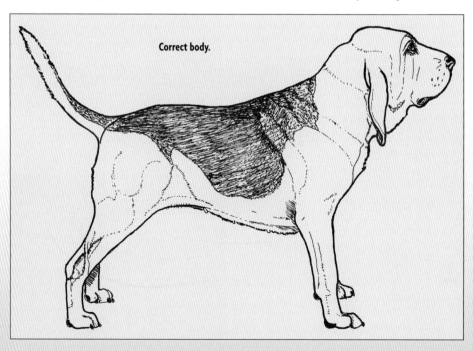

Correct body.

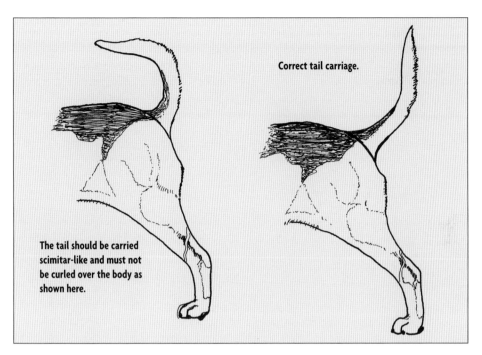

Correct tail carriage.

The tail should be carried scimitar-like and must not be curled over the body as shown here.

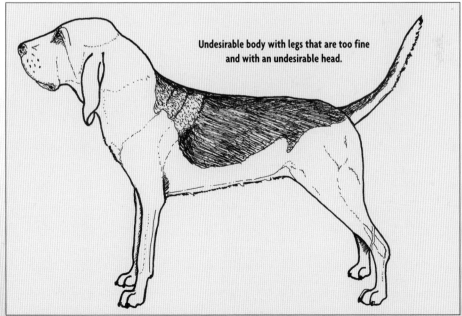

Undesirable body with legs that are too fine and with an undesirable head.

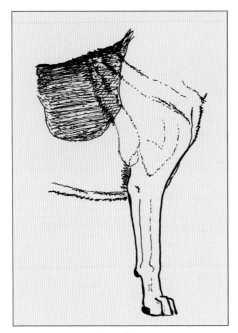

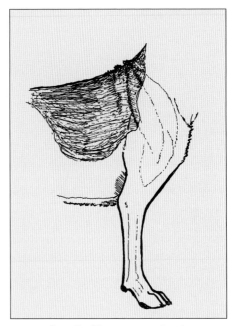

Correct front.

Incorrect front. Shoulder too steep and weak pastern.

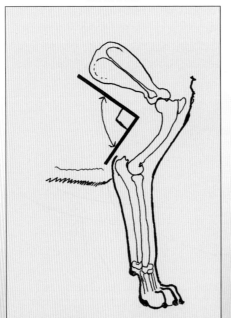

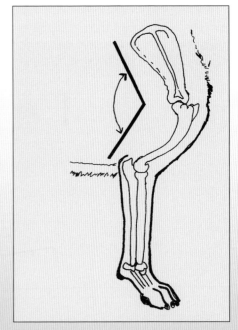

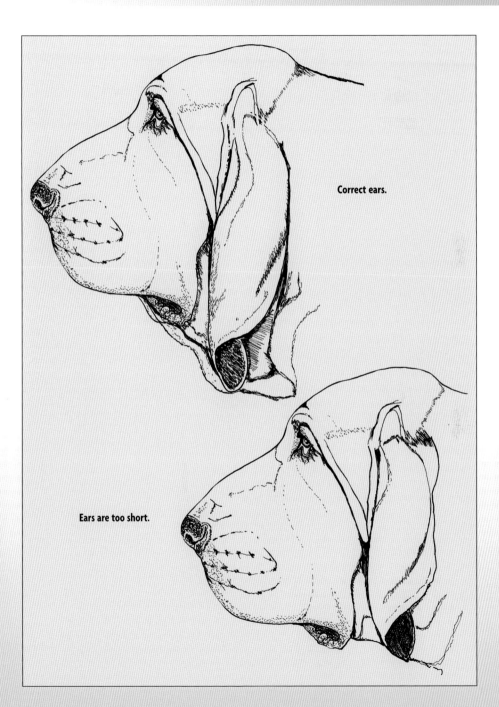

Correct ears.

Ears are too short.

BLOODHOUND

ADDING A BLOODHOUND TO YOUR FAMILY

Living with a dog, especially a Bloodhound, is a major life-altering decision, one that should be researched with at least as much diligence as shopping for a new home, car or major appliance. Give yourself this short quiz to see if you are truly prepared to share your life with a Bloodhound.

Why do you desire this particular breed of dog? There are about 330 recognized breeds of pure-bred dog available, about half of which can be readily found in the US and in some European countries. You have selected this large scenthound because it possesses unique qualities beyond those of all the other breeds you have investigated. A Bloodhound is truly the right animal for you, your family and your living situation. You are committed to providing this Bloodhound puppy with an ideal life.

Do you fully understand the animal, its temperament and its physical and emotional needs? (Yes, dogs definitely have emotional needs.) Have you read as much as possible on the breed to learn the advantages and disadvantages of living with this dog? You can also attend dog shows and trailing events if possible, to better acquaint yourself with members of the breed and talk to the exhibitors and owners about their dogs.

Do you have the time, facilities and funds to support this breed of dog? You will need a house, large garden area, good fencing, time for walks, canine hygiene and exercise, and money for food, veterinary care and

SOME DAM ATTITUDE

When selecting a puppy, be certain to meet the dam of the litter. The temperament of the dam is often predictive of the temperament of her puppies. However, dams occasionally are very protective of their young, some to the point of being testy or aggressive with visitors, whom they may view as a danger to their babies. Such attitudes are more common when the pups are very young and still nursing and should not be mistaken for actual aggressive temperament. If possible, visit the dam away from her pups to make friends with her and gain a better understanding of her true personality.

FINDING A QUALIFIED BREEDER

Before you begin your puppy search, ask for references from your veterinarian and perhaps other breeders to refer you to someone they believe is reputable. Responsible breeders usually raise only one or two breeds of dog. Avoid any breeder who has several different breeds or has several litters at the same time. Dedicated breeders are usually involved with a breed or other dog club. Many participate in some sport or activity related to their breed. Just as you want to be assured of the breeder's qualifications, the breeder wants to be assured that you will make a worthy owner. Expect the breeder to interview you, asking questions about your goals for the pup, your experience with dogs and what kind of home you will provide.

emergency medical treatment if necessary. Strong fencing is especially essential, since most Bloodhounds are either climbers or diggers and will do either or both in order to follow their noses.

What are your goals for the dog and will you be able to achieve them? You have considered whether your Bloodhound will be just a family pet or if you have some type of competition like conformation or obedience in mind. Perhaps you have also considering the possibility of

entering the dog in man-trailing events like tracking, search and rescue for law enforcement or search and rescue as a volunteer. Since the Bloodhound is such a talented animal, you must consider giving the dog ample opportunity to "be all that he can be."

And finally, if all these answers are in the affirmative, how do you find the right dog or puppy?

LOCATING A BREEDER

Finding a good breeder is the first key to success in living with any breed of dog. The only source for a puppy is a breeder who specializes in Bloodhounds, whether you purchase a puppy directly from the breeder or decide to acquire a dog from a rescue scheme at a breeder's kennel. Reputable breeders raise puppies because they know and love their chosen

Let your children participate in the selection of a puppy. This adorable pair of puppies is doing a fine job of beguilng this handsome youngster.

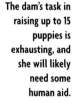

THE BLOODHOUND LITTER
There is considerable variation in the size of a Bloodhound dam's litter. The average litter size can range from a small litter of 4 or 5 pups to as many as 15. A litter of 9 or 10 is common.

breed, and the puppies' welfare is their top priority. They spend considerable time socializing their puppies to prepare them for life outside the whelping box. They also are very discriminating about the people who buy their pups and require assurance that each new owner will provide a happy, healthy environment for their Bloodhound babies. Thus, when searching for a pup, you should expect a good breeder to ask you as many questions as you ask of him. If he makes no enquires

about you or your intentions, move forward and continue looking elsewhere until you find a knowledgeable breeder who cares about his puppies more than your money. The American Kennel Club, veterinarian in your area, dog shows and breed clubs are all good sources to check when looking for a pup of any breed.

FINDING AND SELECTING A BLOODHOUND PUPPY
Be sure to ask any breeder you interview about the health of his puppies, and if the sire and dam have proper certificates of clearance. Ask to see those papers as well as the American Kennel Club registration papers and the puppy's pedigree (essentially the family tree of the dog).

Scrutinize the pup's environment for cleanliness, stimuli and human contact. A dark corner in the basement is not an appropriate

The dam's task in raising up to 15 puppies is exhausting, and she will likely need some human aid.

place to raise a litter of pups. Make sure the pups have received their first distemper shot. Puppies should remain with their dam until they are at least seven weeks of age; good breeders seldom send puppies home before that time. Some breeders of show puppies may want to hold their pups a little longer in order to better evaluate those pups with show potential.

Look for heavy bones, big, tight feet, clear eyes and nose, long ears that reach to the tip of the nose, a square lip and prominent loose skin around the head and neck. If you are looking for a man-trailing Bloodhound, arrange for the breeder to help you test the pups to find the best nose in the litter. After spending seven weeks raising and observing his Bloodhound brood, the breeder should be able to identify which of the pups usually is first to put its head down to sniff and search for its mother or its food dish.

A COMMITTED NEW OWNER
By now you should understand what makes the Bloodhound a most unique and special dog, one that will fit nicely into your family and lifestyle. If you have researched breeders, you should be able to recognize a knowledge-able and responsible Bloodhound breeder who cares not only about his pups but also about what kind of owner you will be. If you have

PEDIGREE VS. REGISTRATION CERTIFICATE
Too often new owners are confused between these two important documents. Your puppy's pedigree, essentially a family tree, is a written record of a dog's genealogy for three generations or more. The pedigree will show you the names as well as performance titles of all dogs in your pup's background. Your breeder must provide you with a registration application, with his part properly filled out. You must complete the application and send it to the AKC with the proper fee. Every puppy must come from a litter that has been AKC-registered by the breeder, born in the US and from a sire and dam that are also registered with the AKC.

The seller must provide you with complete records to identify the puppy. The AKC requires that the seller provide the buyer with the following: breed; sex, color and markings; date of birth; litter number (when available); names and registra-tion numbers of the parents; breeder's name; and date sold or delivered.

completed the final step in your new journey, you have found a litter, or possibly two, of quality Bloodhound pups.

A visit with the puppies and their breeder should be an education in itself. Breed research, breeder selection and puppy visitation are very important

NEW RELEASES

Most breeders release their puppies between seven to ten weeks of age. A breeder who allows puppies to leave the litter at five or six weeks of age may be more concerned with profit than with the puppies' welfare. However, some breeders of show or working breeds may hold one or more top-quality puppies longer, occasionally until three or four months of age, in order to evaluate the puppy's career or show potential and decide which one(s) they will keep for themselves.

aspects of finding the puppy of your dreams. Beyond that, these things also lay the foundation for a successful future with your pup. Puppy personalities within each litter vary, from the shy and easygoing puppy to the one who is dominant and assertive, with most pups falling somewhere in between. By spending time with the puppies, you will be able to recognize certain behaviors and what these behaviors indicate about each pup's temperament. Which type of pup will complement your family dynamics is best determined by observing the puppies in action within their "pack." Your breeder's expertise and recommendations are also valuable. Although you may fall in love with a bold and brassy male, the breeder may suggest that another pup would be best for you. The breeder's experience in rearing Bloodhound pups and matching their temperaments with appropriate humans offers the best assurance that your pup will meet your needs and expectations. The type of puppy that you select is just as important as your decision that the Bloodhound is the breed for you.

The decision to live with a Bloodhound is a serious commitment and not one to be taken lightly. This puppy is a living sentient being that will be dependent on you for basic survival for his entire life. Beyond

Finding the Bloodhound puppy of your dreams will make the search well worth the effort. Discuss your intentions for the puppy with the breeder as you pursue your dream pup.

the basics of survival—food, water, shelter and protection—he needs much, much more. The new pup needs love, nurturing and a proper canine education to mold him into a responsible, well-behaved canine citizen. Your Bloodhound's health and good manners will need consistent monitoring and regular "tune-ups." So your job as a responsible dog owner will be ongoing throughout every stage of his life. If you are not prepared to accept these responsibilities and commit to them for the next decade, likely longer, then you are not prepared to own a dog of any breed.

Although the responsibilities of owning a dog may at times tax your patience, the joy of living with your Bloodhound far outweighs the workload, and a well-mannered adult dog is worth your time and effort. Before your very eyes, your new charge will grow up to be your most loyal friend, devoted to you uncondi- tionally.

PET INSURANCE

Just as you can insure your car, your house and your own health, you likewise can insure your dog's health. Investigate a pet insurance policy by talking to your vet. Depending on the age of your dog, the breed and the kind of coverage you desire, your policy can be very affordable. Most policies cover accidental injuries, poisoning and thousands of medical problems and illnesses, including cancers. Some carriers also offer routine care and immunization coverage.

often preferred to plastic bowls since they sterilize better and pups are less inclined to chew on the metal. Heavy-duty ceramic bowls are popular, but consider how often you will have to pick up those heavy bowls! Buy adult-sized pans, as your puppy will grow into them before you know it.

THE DOG CRATE

If you think that crates are tools of punishment and confinement for when a dog has misbehaved, think again. Most breeders and almost all trainers recommend a crate as the preferred house-training aid as well as for all-around puppy training and safety. Because dogs are natural den creatures that prefer cave-like environments, the benefits of crate use are many. The crate provides the puppy with his very own "safe house," a cozy place to sleep, take a break or seek comfort with a favorite toy; a travel aid to house your dog when on the road, at motels or at the

Your new Bloodhound puppy will spend many a fascinating hour getting to know each family member.

YOUR BLOODHOUND SHOPPING LIST

Just as expectant parents prepare a nursery for their baby, so should you ready your home for the arrival of your Bloodhound pup. If you have the necessary puppy supplies purchased and in place before he comes home, it will ease the puppy's transition from the warmth and familiarity of his mom and littermates to the brand-new environment of his new home and human family. You will be too busy to stock up and prepare your house after your pup comes home, that's for sure! Imagine how a pup must feel upon being transported to a strange new place. It's up to you to comfort him and to let your little pup know that he is going to be happy with you!

FOOD AND WATER BOWLS

Your puppy will need separate bowls for his food and water. Stainless steel pans are generally

THE FIRST FAMILY MEETING

Your puppy's first day at home should be quiet and uneventful. Despite his wagging tail, he is still wondering where his mom and siblings are! Let him make friends with other members of the family on his own terms; don't overwhelm him. You have a lifetime ahead to get to know each other!

ROCK-A-BYE BEDDING

The wide assortment of dog beds today can make your choice quite difficult, as there are many adorable novelty beds in fun styles and prints. It's wise to wait until your puppy has outgrown the chewing stage before providing him with a dog bed, since he might make confetti out of it. Your puppy will be happy with an old towel or blanket in his crate until he is old enough to resist the temptation to chew up his bed. For a dog of any age, a bed with a washable cover is always a wise choice.

vet's office; a training aid to help teach your puppy proper toileting habits; a place of solitude when non-dog people happen to drop by and don't want a lively puppy—or even a well-behaved adult dog— saying hello or begging for attention.

Crates come in several types, although the wire crate and the fiberglass airline-type crate are the most popular. Both are safe and your puppy will adjust to either one, so the choice is up to you. The wire crates offer better visibility for the pup as well as better ventilation. Many of the wire crates easily collapse into suitcase-size carriers. The fiberglass crates, similar to those used by the airlines for animal transport, are sturdier and more den-like, but do not collapse and

are less ventilated than a wire crate, which can be problematic in hot weather. Some of the newer crates are made of heavy plastic mesh; these are very lightweight and fold up into slim-line suitcases. However, a mesh crate might not be suitable for a pup with manic chewing habits. Don't bother with a puppy-sized crate. Although your Bloodhound will be a wee fellow when you bring him home, he will grow up in the blink of an eye and your puppy crate will be useless. Purchase a crate that will accommodate an adult Bloodhound. He will stand about 25 or more inches when full grown, so a large-sized crate will be necessary.

Your local pet shop should have a variety of crates from which you can choose, though it may be necessary for the shop to order an extra-large model for your Bloodhound.

BEDDING AND CRATE PADS

Your puppy will enjoy some type of soft bedding in his "room" (the crate), something he can snuggle into and feel cozy and secure with. Old towels or blankets are good choices for a young pup, since he may (and probably will) have a toileting accident or two in the crate or decide to chew on the bedding material. Once he is fully trained and out of the early chewing stage, you can replace the puppy bedding with a permanent crate pad if you prefer. Crate pads and other dog beds run the gamut from inexpensive to high-end doggie-designer styles, but don't splurge on the good stuff until you are sure that your puppy is reliable and won't tear it up or make a mess on it.

PUPPY TOYS

Just as infants and children require objects to stimulate their minds and bodies, puppies need

> **TOYS 'R SAFE**
> The vast array of tantalizing puppy toys is staggering. Stroll through any pet shop or pet-supply outlet and you will see that the choices can be overwhelming. However, not all dog toys are safe or sensible. Most very young puppies enjoy soft woolly toys that they can snuggle with and carry around. (You know they have outgrown them when they shred them up!) Avoid toys that have buttons, tabs or other enhancements that can be chewed off and swallowed. Soft toys that squeak are fun, but make sure your puppy does not disembowel the toy and remove (and swallow) the squeaker. Toys that rattle or make noise can excite a puppy, but these present the same danger as the squeaky kind and so require supervision. Hard rubber toys that bounce can also entertain a pup, but make sure the size of the toy is Bloodhound-appropriate.

toys to entertain their curious brains, wiggly paws and achy teeth. A fun array of safe doggie toys will help satisfy your puppy's chewing instincts and distract him from gnawing on the leg of your antique chair or your new leather sofa. Most puppy toys are cute and look like they would be a lot of fun, but not all are necessarily safe or good for your puppy, so use caution when you go puppy-toy shopping.

Although Bloodhounds are not

Puppies learn good manners and behavior from their dam.

MAKE A COMMITMENT

Dogs are most assuredly a human's best friend, but they are also a lot of work. When you add a puppy to your family, you also are adding to your daily responsibilities for the next 10 to 15 years. Dogs need more than just food, water and a place to sleep. They also require training (which can be ongoing throughout the lifetime of the dog), activity to keep him physically and mentally fit and hands-on attention every day, plus grooming and health care. Your life as you now know it may well disappear! Are you prepared for such drastic changes?

known to be voracious chewers like many other dogs, they still love to chew. The best "chewcifiers" are nylon and hard rubber bones, which are safe to gnaw on and come in sizes appropriate for all age groups and breeds. Be especially careful of the softer natural bones, which can splinter or develop dangerous sharp edges; pups can easily swallow or choke on those bone splinters. Veterinarians often tell of surgical nightmares involving bits of splintered bone, because in addition to the danger of choking, the sharp pieces can damage the intestinal tract.

Similarly, rawhide chews, while a favorite of most dogs and puppies, can be equally dangerous. Pieces of rawhide are easily swallowed after they get all gummy from chewing, and dogs have been known to choke on large pieces of ingested rawhide. Rawhide chews should be offered only when you can supervise the puppy.

Soft woolly toys are special puppy favorites. They come in a wide variety of cute shapes and sizes; some look like little stuffed animals. Puppies love to shake them up and toss them about, or simply carry them around. Be careful of fuzzy toys that have button eyes or noses that your pup could chew off and swallow, and make sure that he does not "disembowel" a squeaky toy to remove the squeaker! Braided rope toys are similar in that they are fun to chew and toss around, but they shred easily and the strings

Don't forget the toys! Don't wait until your puppy finds his own objects to play with. Provide him with safe chew toys that will distract him from eating your possessions.

Choose safe toys for your Bloodhound. Always monitor his playtime with soft toys.

are easy to swallow. The strings are not digestible and, if the puppy doesn't pass them in his stool, he could end up at the vet's office. As with rawhides, your puppy should be closely monitored with rope toys.

If you believe that your pup has ingested one of these forbidden objects, check his stools for the next couple of days to see whether he passes them when he defecates. At the same time, also watch for signs of intestinal

Dog shows are great places for owners to shop. Many new and innovative products are for sale by vendors.

distress. A call to your veterinarian might be in order to get his advice and be on the safe side.

An all-time favorite toy for puppies (young and old!) is the empty gallon milk jug. Hard plastic juice containers—46 ounces or more—are also excellent. Such containers make lots of noise when they are batted about and puppies go crazy with delight as they play with them. However, they don't often last very long, so be sure to remove and replace them when they get chewed up on the ends. A word of caution about homemade toys: be careful with your choices of non-traditional play objects. Never use old shoes or socks, since a puppy cannot distinguish between the old ones on which he's allowed to chew and the new ones in your closet that are strictly off-limits. That principle applies to anything that resembles something that you don't want your puppy to chew up.

COLLARS

A lightweight nylon collar is the best choice for a very young pup. Quick-clip collars are easy to put on and remove, and they can be adjusted as the puppy grows. Introduce him to his collar as soon as he comes home to get him accustomed to wearing it. He'll get used to it quickly and won't mind

COLLARING OUR CANINES

The standard flat collar with a buckle or a snap, in leather, nylon or cotton, is widely regarded as the everyday all-purpose collar. If the collar fits correctly, you should be able to fit two fingers between the collar and the dog's neck. Such a flat collar is suitable for most breeds of dogs, but greyhound-like dogs (with slender skulls and necks) and thick-necked dogs can easily back out of a collar.

Leather Buckle Collars

Limited-Slip Collar

The martingale, greyhound or limited-slip collar is preferred by many dog owners and trainers. It is fixed with an extra loop that tightens when pressure is applied to the leash. The martingale collar gets tighter but does not "choke" the dog. The limited-slip collar should only be used for walking and training, not for free play or interaction with another dog. These types of collar should never be left on the dog, as the extra loop can lead to accidents.

Choke collars, usually made of stainless steel, are made for training purposes, though are not recommended for small dogs or heavily coated breeds. The chains can injure small dogs or damage long/abundant coats. Thin nylon choke leads are commonly used on show dogs while in the ring, though these are not practical for everyday use.

The harness, with two or three straps that attach over the dog's shoulders and around his torso, is a humane and safe alternative to the conventional collar. By and large, a well-made harness is virtually escape-proof. Harnesses are available in nylon and mesh and can be outfitted on most dogs, ranging from chest girths of 10 to 30 inches.

Snap Bolt Choke Collar

Harness

Nylon Collar

Quick-Click Closure

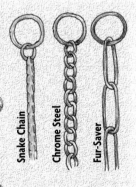

Snake Chain Chrome Steel Fur-Saver

Choke Chain Collars

A head collar, composed of a nylon strap that goes around the dog's muzzle and a second strap that wraps around his neck, offers the owner better control over his dog. This device is recommended for problem-solving with dogs (including jumping up, pulling and aggressive behaviors), but must be used with care.

A training halter, including a flat collar and two straps, made of nylon and webbing, is designed for walking. There are several on the market; some are more difficult to put on the dog than others. The halter harness, with two small slip rings at each end, is recommended for ease of use.

Leash Life

Dogs love leashes! Believe it or not, most dogs dance for joy every time their owners pick up their leashes. The leash means that the dog is going for a walk—and there are few things more exciting than that! Here are some of the kinds of leashes that are commercially available.

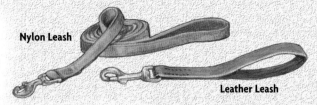

Nylon Leash

Leather Leash

Traditional Leash: Made of cotton, nylon or leather, this is usually about 6 feet in length. A quality-made leather leash is softer on the hands than a nylon one. Durable woven cotton is a popular option. Lengths can vary up to about 48 feet, designed for different uses.

Chain Leash: Usually a metal chain leash with a plastic handle. This is not the best choice for most breeds, as it is heavier than other leashes and difficult to manage.

Retractable Leash: A long nylon cord is housed in a plastic device for extending and retracting. This leash, also known as a flexible leash, is ideal for taking trained dogs for long walks in open areas, although it is not advised for large, powerful breeds. Different lengths and sizes are available, so check that you purchase one appropriate for your dog's weight.

Elastic Leash: A nylon leash with an elastic extension. This is useful for well-trained dogs, especially in conjunction with a head halter. Avoid leashes that are completely elastic, as they afford minimal control to the handler.

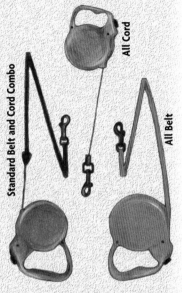

Standard Belt and Cord Combo

All Cord

All Belt

Retractable Leashes

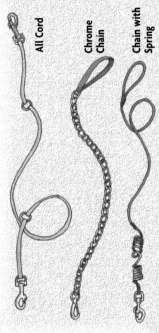

All Cord

Chrome Chain

Chain with Spring

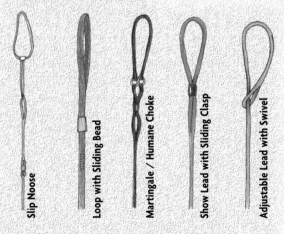

Slip Noose

Loop with Sliding Bead

Martingale / Humane Choke

Show Lead with Sliding Clasp

Adjustable Lead with Swivel

A Variety of Collar-Leash-in-One Products

Adjustable Leash: This has two snaps, one on each end, and several metal rings. It is handy if you need to tether your dog temporarily, but is never to be used with a choke collar.

Tab Leash: A short leash (4 to 6 inches long) that attaches to your dog's collar. This device serves like a handle, in case you have to grab your dog while he's exercising off lead. It's ideal for "half-trained" dogs or dogs that only listen half the time.

Slip Leash: Essentially a leash with a collar built in, similar to what a dog-show handler uses to show a dog. This British-style collar has a ring on the end so that you can form a slip collar. Useful if you have to catch your own runaway dog or a stray.

a bit. Make sure that it is snug enough that it won't slip off, yet loose enough to be comfortable for the pup. You should be able to slip two fingers between the collar and his neck. Check the collar often, as puppies grow in spurts and his collar can become too tight almost overnight. Choke collars are for training purposes only and should never be used on a puppy under four or five months old and worn *only* for training.

LEASHES

A 6-foot nylon lead is an excellent choice for a young puppy. It is lightweight and not as tempting to chew as a leather lead. You can switch to a 6-foot leather lead after your pup has grown and is used to walking politely on a lead. For initial puppy walks and house-training purposes you should invest in a shorter lead so that you have more control over the puppy. At first, you don't want him wandering too far away from you, and when taking him out for toileting you will want to keep him in the specific area chosen for his potty spot.

Once the puppy is heel trained with a traditional leash, you can consider purchasing a retractable lead. A flexible lead is excellent for walking adult dogs that are already leash-wise. The "flexi" allows the dog to roam farther away from you and explore a wider area when out walking, and

TOXIC PLANTS

Plants are natural puppy magnets, but many can be harmful, even fatal, if ingested by a puppy or adult dog. Scout your yard and home interior and remove any plants, bushes or flowers that could be even mildly dangerous. It could save your puppy's life. You can obtain a complete list of toxic plants from your veterinarian, at the public library or by looking online.

also retracts when you need to keep him close to you.

HOME SAFETY FOR YOUR PUPPY

The importance of puppy-proofing cannot be overstated. In addition to making your house comfortable before your Bloodhound's arrival, you also must make sure that your house is safe for your puppy before you bring him home. There are countless hazards in the

A Dog-Safe Home

The dog-safety police are taking you and your new puppy on a house tour. Let's go room by room and see how safe your own home is for your new pup. The following items are doggie dangers, so either they must be removed or the dog should be monitored or not have access to these areas.

Living Room

- house plants (some varieties are poisonous)
- fireplace or wood-burning stove
- paint on the walls (lead-based paint is toxic)
- lead drapery weights (toxic lead)
- lamps and electrical cords
- carpet cleaners or deodorizers

Outdoor

- swimming pool
- pesticides
- toxic plants
- lawn fertilizers

Bathroom

- blue water in the toilet bowl
- medicine cabinet (filled with potentially deadly bottles)
- soap bars, bleach, drain cleaners, etc.
- tampons

Kitchen

- household cleaners in the kitchen cabinets
- glass jars and canisters
- sharp objects (like kitchen knives, scissors and forks)
- garbage can (with remnants of good-smelling things like onions, potato skins, apple or pear cores, peach pits, coffee beans, etc.)

Garage

- antifreeze
- fertilizers (including rose foods)
- pesticides and rodenticides
- pool supplies (chlorine and other chemicals)
- oil and gasoline in containers
- sharp objects, electrical cords and power tools

GOOD CHEWING

Chew toys run the gamut from rawhide chews to hard sterile bones and everything in between. Rawhides are all-time favorites, but they can cause choking when they become mushy from repeated chewing, causing them to break into small pieces that are easy to swallow. Rawhides are also highly indigestible, so many vets advise limiting rawhide treats. Hard sterile bones are great for plaque prevention as well as chewing satisfaction. Dispose of them when the ends become sharp or splintered.

owner's personal living environment that a pup can sniff, chew, swallow or destroy. Many are obvious; others are not. Do a thorough advance house check to remove or rearrange those things that could hurt your puppy, keeping any potentially dangerous items out of areas to which he will have access.

Electrical cords are especially dangerous, since puppies view them as irresistible chew toys. Unplug and remove all exposed cords or fasten them beneath a baseboard where the puppy cannot reach them. Veterinarians and firefighters can tell you horror stories about electrical burns and house fires that originated from puppy-chewed electrical cords. Consider this a most serious precaution for your puppy and the rest of your family.

Scout your home for tiny objects that might be seen at a pup's eye level. Keep medication bottles and cleaning supplies well out of reach, and do the same with waste baskets and other trash containers. It goes without saying that you should not use rodent poison or other toxic chemicals in any puppy area, and that you must keep such containers safely locked up. You will be amazed at how many places a curious puppy can discover!

Once your house has cleared inspection, check your yard. A sturdy fence, well embedded into the ground, will give your dog a safe place to play and potty. Although Bloodhounds are not known to be climbers or fence

If you don't invest in safe chew toys for your Bloodhound, he'll improvise with objects that can be harmful.

Nothing is free of your Bloodhound's nose. Inspect your grounds carefully for hazards and harmful fauna.

jumpers, they are still athletic dogs, so a 5- to 6-foot-high fence should be adequate to contain an agile youngster or adult. Check the fence periodically for necessary repairs. If there is a weak link or space to squeeze through, you can be sure a determined Bloodhound will discover it.

The garage and shed can be hazardous places for a pup, as things like fertilizers, chemicals and tools are usually kept there. It's best to keep these areas off-limits to the pup. Antifreeze is especially dangerous to dogs, as they find the taste appealing and it only takes a few licks from the driveway to kill a dog regardless of its age or size.

VISITING THE VETERINARIAN

A good veterinarian is your Bloodhound puppy's best healthinsurance policy. If you do not already have a veterinarian,

ask friends and experienced dog people in your area for recommendations so that you can select a vet before you bring your Bloodhound puppy home. Also arrange for your puppy's first veterinary examination beforehand, since many vets have two- and three-week waiting periods, and your puppy should visit the veterinarian within a day or so of coming home.

It's important to make sure your puppy's first visit to the veterinarian is a pleasant and positive one. The veterinarian should take great care to befriend the pup and handle him gently to make their first meeting a positive experience. The veterinarian will give the pup a thorough physical examination and set up a schedule for vaccinations and other

THE WORRIES OF MANGE

Sometimes called "puppy mange," demodectic mange is passed to the puppy through the mother's milk. These microscopic mites take up residence in the puppy's hair follicles and sebaceous glands. Stress can cause the mites to multiply, causing bare patches on the face, neck and front legs. If neglected, it can lead to secondary bacterial infections, but if diagnosed and treated early, demodectic mange can be localized and controlled. Most pups recover without complications.

ARE VACCINATIONS NECESSARY?

Vaccinations are recommended for all puppies by the American Veterinary Medical Association (AVMA). Some vaccines are absolutely necessary, while others depend upon a dog's or puppy's individual exposure to certain diseases or the animal's immune history. According to the law, rabies vaccinations are required in all 50 states. Some diseases are fatal while others are treatable, making the need for vaccinating against the latter questionable. Follow your veterinarian's recommendations to keep your dog fully immunized and protected. You can also review the AVMA directive on vaccinations on their website: www.avma.org.

necessary wellness visits. Be sure to show your veterinarian any health and inoculation records, which you should have received from your breeder. Your veterinarian is a great source of canine health information, so be sure to ask questions and take notes. Creating a health journal for your puppy will make a handy reference for his wellness and any future health problems that may arise.

MEETING THE FAMILY

Your Bloodhound's homecoming is an exciting time for all members of the family, and it's only natural that everyone will be eager to meet him, pet him and play with him. However, for the puppy's sake, it's best to make these initial family meetings as uneventful as possible, so that the pup is not over-whelmed with too much, too soon. Remember, he has just left his dam and his littermates and is away from the breeder's home for the first time. Despite his happily wagging tail, he is still apprehensive and wondering where he is and who all these strange humans are. It's best to let him explore on his own and meet the family members as he feels comfortable. Let him investigate all the new

The Bloodhound's large ears can be a hindrance to the hungry hound. Be sure to clean your dog's ears after he has eaten or drunk.

smells, sights and sounds at his own pace. Children should be especially careful to not get overly excited, use loud voices or hug the pup too tightly. Be calm, gentle and affectionate, and be ready to comfort him if he appears frightened or uneasy.

Be sure to show your puppy his new crate during this first day home. Toss a treat or two inside the crate; if he associates the crate with food, he will associate the crate with good things. If he is comfortable with the crate, you can offer him his first meal inside it. Leave the door ajar so he can wander in and out as he chooses.

FIRST NIGHT IN HIS NEW HOME

So much has happened in your Bloodhound puppy's first day away from the breeder. He had his first car ride to his new home. He's met his new human family and perhaps the other family pets. He has explored his new house and yard, at least those places where he is to be allowed during his first weeks at home. He may have visited his new veterinarian. He has eaten his first meal or two away from his dam and littermates. Surely that's enough to tire out an eight-week-old Bloodhound pup—or so you hope!

It's bedtime. During the day the pup will have investigated his crate, which is his new den and sleeping space, so it is not entirely strange to him. Line the crate with a soft towel or blanket that he can snuggle into and gently place him in the crate for the night. Some breeders send home a piece of

Socializing your Bloodhound pup means giving him a variety of experiences to make him well rounded in the company of other dogs and people.

THE CRITICAL SOCIALIZATION PERIOD

Canine research has shown that a puppy's 8th through 16th week is the most critical learning period of his life. This is when the puppy "learns to learn," a time when he needs positive experiences to build confidence and stability. Puppies who are not exposed to different people and situations outside the home during this period can grow up to be fearful and sometimes aggressive. This is also the best time for puppy lessons, since he has not yet acquired any bad habits that could undermine his ability to learn.

bedding from where the pup slept with his littermates, and those familiar scents are a great comfort for the puppy on his first night without his siblings.

He will probably whine or cry. The puppy is objecting to the confinement and the fact that he is alone for the first time. This can be a stressful time for you as well as for the pup. It's important that you remain strong and don't let the puppy out of his crate to comfort him. He will fall asleep eventually. If you release him, the puppy will learn that crying means "out" and will continue that habit. You are laying the groundwork for future habits. Some breeders find that soft music can soothe a crying pup and help him get to sleep.

SOCIALIZING YOUR PUPPY

The next 20 weeks of your Bloodhound puppy's life are the most important of his entire lifetime. A properly socialized puppy will grow up to be a confident and stable adult who will be a pleasure to live with and a welcome addition to the neighborhood.

The importance of socialization cannot be overemphasized. Research on canine behavior has proven that puppies who are not exposed to new sights, sounds, people and animals during their first 20 weeks of life will grow up to be timid and fearful, even aggressive, and unable to flourish away from their familiar home environment.

Socializing your puppy is not difficult and, in fact, will be a fun time for you both. Lead training goes hand in hand with socialization, so your puppy will be learning how to walk on a lead at the same time that he's meeting the neighborhood. Because the Bloodhound is a such a terrific breed, your puppy will enjoy being "the new kid on the block." Take him for short walks, to the park and to other dog-friendly places where he will encounter new people, especially children. Puppies automatically recognize children as "little people" and are drawn to play with them. Just make sure that you supervise these meetings and that the children do not get too rough or encourage him to play too hard. An overzealous pup can often nip too hard, frightening the child and in turn making the puppy overly excited. A bad experience in puppyhood can impact a dog for life, so a pup that has a negative experience with a child may grow up to be shy or even aggressive around children.

Take your puppy along on your daily errands. Puppies are natural "people magnets," and most people who see your pup will want to pet him. All of these encounters will help to mold him

Bloodhound puppies have the most interesting conversations.

CREATE A SCHEDULE
Puppies thrive on sameness and routine. Offer meals at the same time each day, take him out at regular times for potty trips and do the same for play periods and outdoor activity. Make note of when your puppy naps and when he is most lively and energetic, and try to plan his day around those times. Once he is house-trained and more predictable in his habits, he will be better able to tolerate changes in his schedule.

---

into a confident adult dog. Likewise, you will soon feel like a confident, responsible dog owner, rightly proud of your handsome Bloodhound.

Be especially careful of your puppy's encounters and experiences during the eight-to-ten-week-old period, which is also called the "fear period." This is a serious imprinting period, and all contact during this time should be gentle and positive. A frightening or negative event could leave a permanent impression that could affect his future behavior if a similar situation arises.

Also make sure that your puppy has received his first and second rounds of vaccinations before you expose him to other dogs or bring him to places that other dogs may frequent. Avoid dog parks and other strange-dog areas until your vet assures you that your puppy is fully immunized and resistant to the diseases that can be passed between canines. Discuss socialization with your breeder, as some breeders recommend socializing the puppy even before he has received all his inoculations, depending on how outgoing the breed or puppy may be.

"Catch me if you can!" Dogs provide the best exercise for one another.

LEADER OF THE PUPPY'S PACK
Like other canines, your puppy needs an authority figure, someone he can look up to and regard as the leader of his "pack." His first pack leader was his dam, who taught him to be polite and not chew too hard on her ears or nip at her muzzle. He learned those same lessons from his littermates. If he played too rough, they cried in pain and stopped the game, which sent an important message to the rowdy puppy.

As puppies play together, they are also struggling to determine who will be the boss. Being pack animals, dogs need someone to be in charge. If a litter of puppies remained together beyond puppyhood, one of the pups would emerge as the strongest one, the one who calls the shots. Once your puppy leaves the pack, he will look intuitively for a new leader. If he does not recognize you as that leader, he will try to assume that position for himself. Of course, it is hard to imagine

your adorable Bloodhound puppy trying to be in charge when he is so small and seemingly helpless. You must remember that these are natural canine instincts. Do not cave in and allow your pup to get the upper "paw"!

Just as socialization is so important during these first 20 weeks, so too is your puppy's early education. He was born without any bad habits. He does not know what is good or bad behavior. If he does things like nipping and digging, it's because he is having fun and doesn't know that humans consider these things as "bad." It's your job to teach him proper puppy manners, and this is the best time to accomplish that—before he has developed bad habits, since it is much more difficult to "unlearn" or correct unacceptable learned behavior than to teach good behavior from the start.

Make sure that all members of the family understand the importance of being consistent

Praise and encourage your Bloodhound puppy when he has done well. Correct him firmly and fairly when he starts to engage in an inappropriate activity, such as nipping or chewing one of your cloths.

when training their new puppy. If you tell the puppy to stay off the sofa, and your daughter allows him to cuddle on the couch to watch her favorite television show, your pup will be confused about what he is and is not allowed to do. Have a family conference before your pup comes home so that everyone understands the basic principles of puppy training and the rules you have set forth for the pup, and agrees to follow them.

The old adage that "an ounce of prevention is worth a pound of cure" is an especially true one when it comes to puppies. It is much easier to prevent inappropriate behavior than it is to change it. It's also easier and less stressful for the pup, since it will keep discipline to a minimum and create a more positive learning environment for him. That, in turn, will also be easier on you! Here are a few commonsense tips to keep your belongings safe and your puppy out of trouble:

- Keep your closet doors closed and your shoes, socks and other apparel off the floor so your puppy can't get at them.
- Keep a secure lid on the trash container or put the trash where your puppy can't dig into it. He can't damage what he can't reach!
- Supervise your puppy at all times to make sure he is not getting into mischief. If he starts to chew the corner of the rug, you can distract him instantly by tossing a toy for him to fetch. You also will be able to whisk him outside when you notice that he is about to piddle on the carpet. If you can't see your puppy, you can't teach or correct his behavior.

SOLVING PUPPY PROBLEMS

CHEWING AND NIPPING
Nipping at fingers and toes is normal puppy behavior. Chewing is also the way that puppies investigate their surroundings. However, you will have to teach your puppy that chewing anything other than his toys is not acceptable. That won't happen overnight and, at times, puppy teeth will test your patience. However, if you allow nipping and chewing to continue, just think about the damage that a mature Bloodhound can do with a full set of adult teeth.

Whenever your puppy nips your hand or fingers, cry out "Ouch!" in a loud voice, which should startle your puppy and stop him from nipping, even if only for a moment. Immediately distract him by offering a small treat or an appropriate toy for him to chew instead (which means having chew toys and puppy treats handy or in your pockets at all times). Praise him when he takes the toy and tell him what a good fellow he is. Praise is just as, or even more, important to puppy training as discipline and correction.

Puppies also tend to nip at children more often than adults, since they perceive little ones to be more vulnerable and more similar to their littermates. Teach your children appropriate responses to nipping behavior and, if they are unable to handle it themselves, you may have to intervene. Puppy nips can be quite painful, and a child's frightened reaction will only encourage a puppy to nip harder, which is a natural canine response. As with all other puppy situations, interaction between your Bloodhound puppy and children should be supervised.

Chewing on objects, not just family members' fingers and ankles, is also normal canine behavior that can be especially tedious (for the owner, not the pup) during the teething period when the puppy's adult teeth are coming in. At this stage, chewing just plain feels good. Furniture legs and cabinet corners are common puppy favorites. Shoes and other personal items also taste pretty good to a pup.

BE CONSISTENT

Consistency is a key element, in fact is absolutely necessary, to a puppy's learning environment. A behavior (such as chewing, jumping up or climbing onto the furniture) cannot be forbidden one day and then allowed the next. That will only confuse the pup and he will not understand what he is supposed to do. Just one or two episodes of allowing an undesirable behavior to "slide" will imprint that behavior on a puppy's brain and make that behavior more difficult to erase or change.

Your Bloodhound puppy depends on you for everything, from his food and water to his education and entertainment.

The best solution is, once again, prevention. If you value something, keep it tucked away and out of reach. You can't hide your dining-room table in a closet, but you can try to deflect the chewing by applying a bitter product made just to deter dogs from chewing. Available in a spray or cream, this substance is vile-tasting, although safe for dogs, and most puppies will avoid the forbidden object after one tiny taste. You also can apply the product to your leather leash if the puppy tries to chew on his lead during leash- training sessions. Keep a ready supply of safe chews handy to offer your Bloodhound as a distraction when he starts to chew on something that's a "no-no." Remember, at this tender age, he does not yet know what is permitted or forbidden, so you

have to be "on call" every minute he's awake and on the prowl. You may lose a treasure or two during puppy's growing-up period, and the furniture could sustain a nasty nick or two. These can be trying times, so be prepared for those inevitable accidents and comfort yourself in knowing that this too shall pass.

PUPPY WHINING

Puppies often cry and whine, just as infants and little children do. It's their way of telling us that they are lonely or in need of attention. Your puppy will miss his litter-mates and will feel insecure when he is left alone. You may be out of the house or just in another room, but he will still feel alone. During these times, the puppy's crate should be his personal comfort station, a place all his own where he can feel safe and secure. Once he learns that being alone is okay and not something to be feared, he will settle down without crying or objecting. You might want to leave a radio on while he is crated, as the sound of human voices can be soothing and will give the impression that people are around.

Give your puppy a favorite toy to entertain him whenever he is crated. You will both be happier: the puppy because he is safe in his den, and you because he is quiet, safe and not getting into puppy escapades that can wreak havoc in your house.

EVERYDAY CARE OF YOUR
BLOODHOUND

Adding a Bloodhound to your household means adding a new family member who will need your care each and every day. When your Bloodhound pup first comes home, you will start a routine with him so that, as he grows up, your dog will have a daily schedule just as you do. The aspects of your dog's daily care will likewise become regular parts of your day, so you'll both have a new schedule. Dogs learn by consistency and they thrive on routine: regular times for meals, exercise, grooming and potty trips are just as important for your dog as they are to you! Your dog's schedule will depend much on your family's daily routine, but remember, you now have a new member of the family who is part of your day, every day!

FEEDING

Feeding your dog the best diet is based on various factors, including age, activity level, overall condition and size of breed. When you visit the breeder, he will share with you his advice about the proper diet for your dog based on his experience with the breed and the foods with which he has had success. Likewise, your vet will be a helpful source of advice throughout the

dog's life and will aid you in planning a diet for optimum health.

FEEDING THE PUPPY

Of course, your pup's very first food will be his dam's milk. There may be special situations in which pups fail to nurse, necessitating that the breeder hand-feed them with a formula, but, for the most part, pups spend the first weeks of life nursing from their dam. The breeder weans the pups by gradually introducing solid foods and decreasing the milk meals. Pups may even start themselves off on the weaning process, albeit inadvertently, if they snatch bites from their mom's food bowl.

By the time the pups are ready for new homes, they are fully weaned and eating a good puppy

Deciding what to feed your growing Bloodhound depends on knowing what he needs to develop properly in body and mind. Feeding affects the dog's growth, behavior and coat quality.

Rely on your breeder's recommendation for the best food to offer your growing Bloodhound pup.

food. As a new owner, you may be thinking, "Great! The breeder has taken care of the hard part!" Not so fast.

A puppy's first year of life is the time when all, or most, of his growth and development takes place. This is a delicate time, and diet plays a huge role in proper skeletal and muscular formation. Improper diet and exercise habits can lead to damaging problems that will compromise the dog's health and movement for his entire life. That being said, new owners should not worry needlessly. With the myriad types of food formulated specifically for growing pups of different-sized breeds, dog-food manufacturers have taken much of the guesswork out of feeding your puppy well. Since growth-food formulas are designed to provide the nutrition that a growing puppy needs, it is unnecessary and, in fact, can prove harmful to add supplements to the diet. Research has shown that too much of certain vitamins and minerals predispose a dog to skeletal problems. It's by no means a case of "if a little is good, a

lot is better!" At every stage of your dog's life, too much or too little in the way of nutrients can be harmful, which is why a manufactured complete food is the easiest way to know that your dog is getting what he needs.

Because of a young pup's small body and accordingly small digestive system, his daily portion will be divided up into small meals throughout the day. This can mean starting off with three or more meals a day and decreasing the number of meals as the pup matures. Eventually you can feed only one meal a day, although it is generally thought that dividing the day's food into two meals on a morning/evening schedule is better for the dog's digestion.

VARIETY IS THE SPICE

Although dog-food manufacturers contend that dogs don't like variety in their diets, studies show quite the opposite to be true. Dogs would much rather vary their meals than eat the same old chow day in and day out. Dry kibble is no more exciting for a dog than the same bowl of bran flakes would be for you. Fortunately, there are dozens of varieties available on the market, and your dog will likely show preference for certain flavors over others. A word of warning: don't overdo it or you'll develop a fussy eater who only wants chopped beef and other delicacies every night.

BARF THE WAY TO BETTER HEALTH

That's Biologically Appropriate Raw Food for your dog, as designed and trademarked by Dr. Ian Billinghurst. An alternative to feeding commercially prepared dog food from a bag or a can that are known to contain numerous additives and preservatives, this diet aims to increase the longevity, overall health and reproductive abilities of dogs. The BARF diet is based on the feeding habits of wild or feral animals and thus includes whole raw animal- and plant-based foods as well as bones. In theory, BARF mimics the natural diets of dogs and contains muscle meat, bone, fat and organ meat plus vegetable matter. Many owners are very successful with the diet and others are not. Next time you visit your vet, ask him about BARF.

Regarding the feeding schedule, feeding the pup at the same times and in the same place each day is important, both for housebreaking purposes and for establishing the dog's everyday routine. As for the amount to feed, growing puppies generally need proportionately more food per body weight than their adult counterparts, but a pup should never be allowed to gain excess weight. Dogs of all ages should be kept in proper body condition, but extra weight can strain a pup's developing frame, causing skeletal problems.

Watch your pup's weight as he grows and, if the recommended amounts seem to be too much or too little for your pup, consult the vet about appropriate dietary changes. Keep in mind that treats, although small, can quickly add up throughout the day, contributing unnecessary calories. Treats are fine when used prudently; opt for dog treats specially formulated to be healthy, or nutritious snacks like small pieces of cheese or cooked chicken.

FEEDING THE ADULT DOG

For the adult (meaning physically mature) dog, feeding properly is about maintenance, not growth. Again, correct weight is a concern. Your dog should appear fit and should have an evident "waist." His ribs should not be protruding (a sign of being underweight), but they should be covered by only a slight layer of fat. Under normal circumstances, an adult dog can be maintained fairly easily with a good, nutritionally complete adult-formula food.

Discuss food choices with your breeder. Rely on his experience with the Bloodhound and don't vary too far from his and your vet's recommendations.

Monitor your Bloodhound's daily food intake to determine the portion and schedule best for your dog.

Factor treats into your dog's overall daily caloric intake, and avoid offering table scraps. Overweight dogs are more prone to health problems. Research has even shown that obesity takes years off a dog's life. With that in mind, resist the urge to overfeed and over-treat. Don't make unnecessary additions to your dog's diet, whether with tidbits or with extra vitamins and minerals.

The amount of food needed for proper maintenance will vary depending on the individual dog's activity level, but you will be able to tell if the daily portions are keeping him in good shape. With the wide variety of good complete foods available, choosing what to feed is largely a matter of personal preference. Just as with the puppy, the adult dog should have consistency in his mealtimes and feeding place. In addition to a consistent routine, regular mealtimes also allow the owner to see how much his dog his eating. If the dog seems never to be satisfied or, likewise, becomes uninterested in his food,

the owner will know right away that something is wrong and can consult the vet.

DIETS FOR THE AGING DOG
A good rule of thumb is that once a dog has reached 75% of his expected lifespan, he has reached "senior citizen" or geriatric status, so your Bloodhound will be considered a senior at seven years of age. Of course, this varies from breed to breed, with the smallest breeds generally enjoying the longest lives and the largest breeds unfortunately being the shortest lived.

What does aging have to do with your dog's diet? No, he won't get a discount at the local diner's early-bird special. Yes, he will require some dietary changes to accommodate the changes that come along with increased age. One change is that the older dog's dietary needs become more similar to those of a puppy. Specifically, dogs can metabolize more protein as youngsters and seniors than in the adult-maintenance stage. Discuss with your vet whether you need to switch to a higher protein or senior-formulated food, or whether your current adult-dog food contains sufficient nutrition for the senior.

Watching the dog's weight remains essential, even more so in the senior stage. Older dogs are already more vulnerable to illness, and obesity only contributes to

their susceptibility to problems. As the older dog becomes less active and thus exercises less, his regular portions may cause him to gain weight. At this point, you may consider decreasing his daily food intake or switching to a reduced-calorie food. As with any other changes, you should consult your vet for advice.

TYPES OF FOOD
AND READING THE LABEL
When selecting the type of food to feed your dog, it is important to check out the label for ingredients. Many dry food products have soybean, corn or rice as the main ingredient. The main ingredient

NOT HUNGRY?
No dog in his right mind would turn down his dinner, would he? If you notice that your dog has lost interest in his food, there could be any number of causes. Dental problems are a common cause of appetite loss, one that is often overlooked. If your dog has a toothache, a loose tooth or sore gums from infection, chances are it doesn't feel so good to chew. Think about when you've had a toothache! If your dog does not approach the food bowl with his usual enthusiasm, look inside his mouth for signs of a problem. Whatever the cause, you'll want to consult your vet so that your chow hound can get back to his happy, hungry self as soon as possible.

will be listed first on the label, with the rest of the ingredients following in descending order according to their proportion in the food. While these types of dry food are fine, you should also look into dry foods based on meat or fish. These are better quality foods and, thus, higher priced. However, they may be just as economical in the long run because studies have shown that it takes less quantity of the higher-quality foods to maintain a dog.

Comparing the various types of food, dry, canned and semi-moist, dry foods contain the least amount of water whereas canned foods contain the most water. Proportionately, dry foods are the most calorie- and nutrient-dense, which means that you need more of a canned food product to supply the same amount of nutrition. For large dogs like Bloodhounds, this can be an issue, since it takes a large volume of canned food to fulfill their nutritional needs. (Smaller breeds do fine on canned foods and, if feeding dry food to a small dog, it is wise to choose a "small bite" formula with pieces that are easier for their small mouths and teeth to handle.) So, while the choice of food type is an individual one based on owner preference and what the dog seems to like, you will most likely be better off with dry or semi-moist foods for your Bloodhound. You may find success mixing the food types as well. Water is important for all dogs, but even more so for those fed dry foods, as there is not a high water content in their food.

There are strict controls that regulate the nutritional content of dog food, and a food has to meet the minimum requirements in order to be considered "complete and balanced." It is important that you choose such a food for your dog, so check the label to be sure that your chosen food meets the require-ments. If not, look for a food that clearly states on the label that it is formulated to be complete and balanced for your dog's particular stage of life.

Recommendations for amounts to feed will also be indicated on the label. You should also ask your vet about proper food portions, and you will keep an eye on your dog's condition to see whether the recommended amounts are adequate. If he becomes over- or underweight, you will need to

make adjustments, and this also would be a good time to consult your vet.

The food label may also make feeding suggestions, such as whether moistening a dry-food product is recommended. Sometimes a splash of water will make the food more palatable for the dog and even enhance the flavor.

Don't be overwhelmed by the many factors that go into feeding your dog. Manufacturers of complete and balanced foods make it easy, and once you find the right food and amounts for your own dog, his daily feeding will be a matter of routine.

DON'T FORGET THE WATER!

For a dog, it's always time for a drink! Regardless of what type of food he eats, there's no doubt that he needs plenty of water. Fresh, cold water, in a clean bowl, should be freely available to your dog at all times. There are special circum-stances, such as during puppy housebreaking, when you will want to monitor your pup's water intake so that you will be able to predict when he will need to relieve himself, but water must be available to him nonetheless. Water is essential for hydration and proper body function, just as it is in humans.

You will get to know how much your dog typically drinks in a day. Of course, in the heat or if

Monitor your pup's water intake during housebreaking. Keep in mind that he can only hold his water for an hour or less.

WHAT IS "BLOAT"?

Need yet another reason to avoid tossing your dog a morsel from your plate? It is shown that dogs fed table scraps have an increased risk of developing bloat or gastric torsion. Did you know that more occurrences of bloat occur in the warm-weather months due to the frequency of outdoor cooking and dining, and dogs' receiving "samples" from the fired-up Weber®.

You likely have heard the term "bloat," which refers to gastric torsion (gastric dilatation/volvulus), a potentially fatal condition. As it is directly related to feeding and exercise practices, a brief explanation here is warranted: The term "dilatation" means that the dog's stomach is filled with air, while "volvulus" means that the stomach is twisted around on itself, blocking the entrance/exit points. Dilatation/volvulus is truly a deadly combination, although they also can occur independently of each other. An affected dog cannot digest food or pass gas, and blood cannot flow to the stomach, causing accumulation of toxins and gas, great pain and shock.

Many theories exist on what exactly causes bloat, but we do know that deep-chested breeds are more prone. Things like eating a large meal, gulping water, strenuous exercise too close to mealtimes or a combination of these can contribute to bloat, though not every case is directly related to these more well-known causes. With that in mind, we can focus on incorporating simple daily preventatives and knowing how to recognize the symptoms. Affected dogs need immediate veterinary attention, as death can result quickly. Signs include obvious restlessness/discomfort, crying in pain, drooling/excessive salivation, unproductive attempts to vomit or relieve himself, visibly bloated appearance and collapsing. Do not wait; get to the vet right away if you see any of these symptoms. The vet will confirm by X-ray if the stomach is bloated with air; if so, the dog must be treated immediately.

A bloated dog will be treated for shock, and the stomach must be relieved of the air pressure as well as surgically returned to its correct position. If part of the stomach wall has died, that part must be removed. Usually the stomach is stapled to the abdominal wall to prevent another episode of bloating; this may or may not be successful. The vet must also check the dog for heart problems related to the condition.

exercising vigorously, he will be more thirsty and will drink more. However, if he begins to drink noticeably more water for no apparent reason, this could signal any of various problems and you are advised to consult your vet.

Water is the best drink for dogs. Some owners are tempted to give milk from time to time or to moisten dry food with milk, but dogs do not have the enzymes necessary to digest the lactose in milk, which is much different from the milk that nursing puppies receive. Therefore stick with clean fresh water to quench your dog's thirst, and always have it readily available to him.

A word of caution concerning your deep-chested dog's water intake: he should never be allowed to gulp water, especially at mealtimes. In fact, his water intake should be limited at mealtimes as a rule. This simple daily precaution can go a long way in protecting your dog from the dangerous and potentially fatal gastric torsion (bloat).

Letting your dog run free in your fenced yard is an ideal way to give your Bloodhound enjoyable, stress-free exercise.

EXERCISE

We all know the importance of exercise for humans, so it should come as no surprise that it is essential for our canine friends as well. Now, regardless of your own level of fitness, get ready to assume the role of personal trainer for your dog. It's not as hard as it sounds, and it will have health benefits for

you, too.

Just as with anything else you do with your dog, you must set a routine for his exercise. It's the same as your going on a run each morning before work or never missing the 7 p.m. aerobics class. If you plan it and get into the habit of actually doing it, it will become just another part of your day. Think of it as making daily exercise appointments with your dog, and stick to your schedule.

As a rule, dogs in normal health should have at least a half-hour of activity each day. Dogs with health or orthopedic problems may have specific limitations and their exercise plans are best devised with the help of a vet. For healthy dogs, there are many ways to fit 30 minutes of activity into your day. Depending on your schedule, you may plan a 15-minute walk or activity session in the morning or again in the evening, or do it all at

TWO'S COMPANY

One surefire method of increasing your adult dog's exercise plan is to adopt a second dog. If your dog is well socialized, he should take to his new canine pal in no time and soon the two will be giving each other lots of activity and exercise as they play, romp and explore together. Most owners agree that two dogs is hardly much more work than one. If you cannot afford a second dog, get together with a friend or neighbor who has a well-trained dog. Your dog will definitely enjoy the company of a new four-legged playmate.

once in a half-hour session each day. Walking is the most popular way to exercise a dog (it's good for you, too!); other suggestions include retrieving games, jogging and Frisbee® or other active games with his toys. If you have a safe body of water nearby and a dog that likes to swim, swimming is an excellent form of exercise for your dog, putting no stress on his frame.

On that note, some precautions should be taken with a puppy's exercise. During his first year, when he is growing and developing, he should not be subject to stressful activity that stresses his body. Short walks at a comfortable pace and play sessions in the yard are good for a growing pup, and his exercise can be increased as he grows up.

For overweight dogs, dietary changes and activity will help the goal of weight loss (Sound familiar?). While they should of course be encouraged to be active, remember not to overdo it as the excess weight is already putting strain on his vital organs and bones. As for active and working dogs, some of them never seem to tire! They will enjoy time spent with their owners doing things together.

Regardless of your dog's condition and activity level, exercise offers benefits to all dogs and owners. Consider the fact that dogs who are kept active are more stimulated both physically and mentally, meaning that they are less likely to become bored and lapse into destructive behavior. Also consider the benefits of one-on-one time with your dog every day, continually strengthening the bond between the two of you. Furthermore, exercising together will improve health and longevity for both of you. Both of you need exercise, and now you both have a workout partner and motivator!

Your local pet shop should have a variety of tools with which you can groom your Bloodhound.

Use a bristle brush, preferably on a daily basis, to keep your Bloodhound's coat shiny and healthy.

GROOMING

BRUSHING

A natural bristle brush or a hound glove can be used for regular routine brushing. Daily brushing is effective for removing dead hair and stimulating the dog's natural oils to add shine and a healthy look to the coat. Although the Bloodhound's coat is hard and close, it does require a five-minute once-over to keep it looking its shiny best. Regular grooming sessions are also a good way to spend time with your dog. Many dogs grow to like the feel of being brushed and will enjoy the daily routine.

Beyond brushing, Bloodhounds have few grooming needs other than caring for their very large, pendulous ears and deep-set eyes. The ears are low-slung and fold about the side of the head, which can lead to rather heavy wax build-up. Just a wipe or two inside the ear will keep them clean, and this should be performed daily or, at the very least, weekly. Many hounds are subject to more waxy ears than others, so regular and frequent ear checks are a good owner policy.

BATHING

In general, dogs need to be bathed only a few times a year, possibly more often if your dog gets into something messy or if he starts to smell like a dog. Show dogs are usually bathed before every show, which could be as frequent as weekly, although this depends on the owner. Bathing too frequently can have negative effects on the skin and coat, removing natural oils and causing dryness.

If you give your dog his first bath when he is young, he will become accustomed to the process. Wrestling a dog into the tub or chasing a freshly shampooed dog who has escaped from the bath will be no fun! Most dogs don't naturally enjoy their baths, but you at least want him to cooperate with you.

Before bathing the dog, have the items you'll need close at hand. First, decide where you will bathe the dog. You should have a tub or basin with a non-slip surface. Small dogs can even be bathed in a sink. In warm weather, some like to use a portable pool in the yard, although

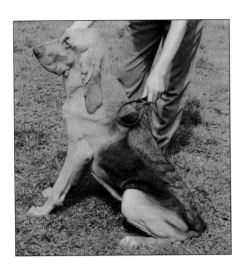

you'll want to make sure your dog doesn't head for the nearest dirt pile following his bath! You will also need a hose or shower spray to wet the coat thoroughly, a shampoo formulated for dogs, absorbent towels and perhaps a blow dryer. Human shampoos are too harsh for dogs' coats and will dry them out.

Before wetting the dog, give him a brush-through to remove any dead hair, dirt and mats. Make sure he is at ease in the tub and have the water at a comfortable temperature. Begin bathing by wetting the coat all the way down to the skin. Massage in the shampoo, keeping it away from his face, ears and eyes. Rinse him thoroughly, again avoiding the eyes and ears, as you don't want to get water in the ear canals. A thorough rinsing is important, as shampoo residue is drying and itchy to the dog. After rinsing, wrap him in a towel to

absorb the initial moisture. You can finish drying with either a towel or a blow dryer on low heat, held at a safe distance from the dog. You should keep the dog indoors and away from drafts until he is completely dry.

NAIL CLIPPING

Having his nails trimmed is not on many dogs' lists of favorite things to do. With this in mind, you will need to accustom your puppy to the procedure at a young age so that he will sit still (well, as still as he can) for his pedicures. Long nails can cause the dog's feet to spread, which is not good for him; likewise, long nails can hurt if they unintentionally scratch, not good for you!

Some dogs' nails are worn down naturally by walking on hard surfaces, so the frequency with which you clip depends on your individual dog. Look at his nails from time to time and clip as needed; a good way to know when it's time for a trim is if you hear

An undercoat rake facilitates the removal of dead hair from the Bloodhound's coat during shedding season. Purchase only top-quality durable grooming tools for use on your Bloodhound.

If you introduce your Bloodhound puppy to the nail clipping routine, you will be blessed with an adult that doesn't mind having his regular pedicure.

Check your dog's nails regularly. If he exercises on rough pavement, you will rarely have to trim his nails.

your dog clicking as he walks across the floor.

There are several types of nail clippers and even electric nail-grinding tools made for dogs; first we'll discuss using the clipper. To start, have your clipper ready and some doggie treats on hand. You want your pup to view his nail-clipping sessions in a positive light, and what better way to convince him than with food? You may want to enlist the help of an assistant to comfort the pup and offer treats as you concentrate on the clipping itself. The guillotine-type clipper is thought of by many as the easiest type to use; the nail tip is inserted into the opening and blades on the top and bottom snip it off in one clip.

Start by grasping the pup's paw; a little pressure on the foot pad causes the nail to extend, making it easier to clip. Clip off a little at a time. If you can see the "quick," which is a blood vessel that runs through each nail, you will know how much to trim, as you do not want to cut into the quick. On that note, if you do cut the quick, which

will cause bleeding, you can stem the flow of blood with a styptic pencil or other clotting agent. If you mistakenly nip the quick, do not panic or fuss, as this will cause the pup to be afraid. Simply reassure the pup, stop the bleeding and move on to the next nail. Don't be discouraged; you will become a professional canine pedicurist with practice.

You may or may not be able to see the quick, so it's best to just clip off a small bit at a time. If you see a dark dot in the center of the nail, this is the quick and your cue to stop clipping. Tell the puppy he's a "good boy" and offer a piece of treat with each nail. You can also use nail-clipping time to examine the footpads, making sure that they are not dry and cracked and that nothing has become embedded in them.

The nail grinder, the second choice, is many owners' first choice. Accustoming the puppy to the sound of the grinder and sensation of the buzz presents fewer challenges than the clipper, and there's no chance of cutting through the quick. Using the grinder on a low setting and always talk soothingly to your dog. He won't mind his salon visit, and he'll have nicely polished nails as well.

EAR CLEANING
While keeping your dog's ears clean unfortunately will not cause him to "hear" your commands any better, it

will protect him from ear infection and ear-mite infestation. In addition, a dog's ears are vulnerable to waxy build-up and to collecting foreign matter from the outdoors. Look in your dog's ears regularly to ensure that they look pink, clean and otherwise healthy. Even if they look fine, an odor in the ears signals a problem and means it's time to call the vet.

A dog's ears should be cleaned regularly; once a week is suggested, and you can do this along with your regular brushing. Using a cotton ball or pad, and never probing into the ear canal, wipe the ear gently. You can use an ear-cleansing liquid or powder available from your vet or pet-supply store, or some owners prefer to use home-made solutions with ingredients like one part white vinegar and one part hydrogen peroxide. Ask your vet about home

remedies before you attempt to concoct something on your own!

Keep your dog's ears free of excess hair by plucking it as needed. If done gently, this will be painless for the dog. Look for wax, brown droppings (a sign of ear mites), redness or any other abnormalities. At the first sign of a problem, contact your vet so that he can prescribe an appropriate medication.

IDENTIFICATION AND TRAVEL

ID FOR YOUR DOG

You love your dog and want to keep him safe. Of course you take every precaution to prevent his escaping from the yard or becoming lost or stolen. You have a sturdy high fence and you always keep your dog on lead when out and about in public places. However, if your dog is not properly identified, you are overlooking a major aspect of his safety. We hope to never be in a situation where our dog is missing, but we should practice prevention in the unfortunate case that this happens; identification greatly increases the chances of your dog's being returned to you

There are several ways to identify your dog. First, the traditional dog tag should be a staple in your dog's wardrobe, attached to his everyday collar. Tags can be made of sturdy plastic and various metals, and should include your contact information so that a person who finds the dog can get in

---

PET OR STRAY?

Besides the obvious benefit of providing your contact information to whoever finds your lost dog, an ID tag makes your dog more approachable and more likely to be recovered. A strange dog wandering the neighborhood without a collar and tags will look like a stray, while the collar and tags indicate that the dog is someone's pet. Even if the ID tags become detached from the collar, the collar alone will make a person more likely to pick up the dog.

touch with you right away to arrange his return. Many people today enjoy the wide range of decorative tags available, so have fun and create a tag to match your dog's personality. Of course, it is important that the tag stays on the collar, so have a secure "O" ring attachment; you also can explore the type of tag that slides right onto the collar.

In addition to the ID tag, which every dog should wear even if identified by another method, two other forms of identification have become popular: microchipping and tattooing. In microchipping, a tiny scannable chip is painlessly inserted under the dog's skin. The number is registered to you so that, if your lost dog turns up at a clinic or shelter, the chip can be scanned to retrieve your contact information.

The advantage of the microchip is that it is a permanent form of ID, but there are some factors to consider. Several different companies make microchips, and not all are compatible with the others' scanning devices. It's best to find a company with a universal microchip that can be read by scanners made by other companies as well. It won't do any good to have the dog chipped if the information cannot be retrieved. Also, not every humane society, shelter and clinic is equipped with a scanner, although more and more facilities are equipping themselves. In fact, many shelters microchip

dogs that they adopt out to new homes.

In the US, there are five or six major microchip manufacturers as well as a few databases. The American Kennel Club's Companion Animal Recovery unit works in conjunction with HomeAgain™ Companion Animal Retrieval System (Schering-Plough). In the UK, The Kennel Club is affiliated with the National Pet Register, operated by Wood Green Animal Shelters.

Because the microchip is not visible to the eye, the dog must wear a tag that states that he is microchipped so that whoever picks him up will know to have him scanned. He of course also should have a tag with contact information in case his chip cannot be read. Humane societies and veterinary clinics offer this service, which is usually very affordable.

Though less popular than microchipping, tattooing is another permanent method of ID for dogs. Most vets perform this service, and there are also clinics that perform dog tattooing. This is also an affordable procedure and one that will not cause much discomfort for the dog. It is best to put the tattoo in a visible area, such as the ear, to deter theft. It is sad to say that there are cases of dogs' being stolen and sold to research laboratories, but such laboratories will not accept tattooed dogs.

To ensure that the tattoo is

effective in aiding your dog's return to you, the tattoo number must be registered with a national organization. This way, when someone finds a tattooed dog, a phone call to the registry will quickly match the dog with his owner.

HITTING THE ROAD

Car travel with your dog may be limited to necessity only, such as trips to the vet, or you may bring your dog along most everywhere you go. This will depend much on your individual dog and how he reacts to rides in the car. You can begin desensitizing your dog to car travel as a pup so that it's something that he's used to. Still, some dogs suffer from motion sickness. Your vet may prescribe a medication for this if trips in the car pose a problem for your dog. At the very least, you will need to get him to the vet, so he will need to tolerate these trips with the least amount of hassle possible.

Start taking your pup on short trips, maybe just around the block to start. If he is fine with short trips, lengthen your rides a little at a time. Start to take him on your errands or just for drives around town. By this time it will be easy to tell if your dog is a born traveler or if he will prefer staying at home when you are on the road.

Of course, safety is a concern for dogs in the car. First, he must travel securely, not left loose to roam about the car where he could

Individual Bloodhounds, both young and adult, differ in regard to how much they like (or dislike) car travel.

be injured or distract the driver. A young pup can be held by a passenger initially but should soon graduate to a travel crate, which can be the same crate he uses in the home. Other options include a car harness (like a seat belt for dogs) and partitioning the back of the car with a gate made for this purpose.

Bring along what you will need for the dog. He should wear his collar and ID tags, of course, and you should bring his leash, water (and food if a long trip) and clean-up materials for potty breaks and in case of motion sickness. Always keep your dog on his leash when you make stops, and never leave him alone in the car. Many a dog has died from the heat inside a closed car; this does not take much time at all. A dog left alone inside a car can also be a target for thieves.

Training a Bloodhound puppy before his hormones "kick in" will make the job of keeping his attention a thousand-fold easier. The combination of curiosity, sexual urges and that amazing nose can complicate an owner's training lessons.

BASIC TRAINING PRINCIPLES: PUPPY VS. ADULT

There's a big difference between training an adult dog and training a young puppy. With a young puppy, everything is new! At eight to ten weeks of age, he will be experiencing many new things, and he has nothing to which to compare these experiences. Up to this point, he has been with his dam and littermates, not one-on-one with people except in his interactions with his breeder and visitors to the litter.

When you first bring the puppy home, he is eager to please you. This means that he accepts doing things your way! During the next couple of months, he will absorb the basis of everything he needs to know for the rest of his life. This early age is even referred to as the "sponge" stage. After that, for the next 18 months, it's up to you to reinforce good manners by building on the foundation that you've established. Once your puppy is reliable in basic commands and behavior, and has reached the appropriate age, you may gradually introduce him to some of the interesting sports, games and activities available to pet owners and their dogs.

Raising your puppy is a family affair. Each member of the family must know what rules to set forth for the puppy and how to use the same one-word commands to mean exactly the same thing every time. Even if yours is a large family, one person will soon be considered by the pup to be the leader, the Alpha person in his pack, the "boss" who must be obeyed. Often that highly regarded person turns out to be the one who feeds the puppy. Food ranks very high on the puppy's list of important things!

CREATURES OF HABIT

Canine behaviorists and trainers aptly describe dogs as "creatures of habit," meaning that dogs respond to structure in their daily lives and welcome a routine. Do not interpret this to mean that dogs enjoy endless repetition in their training sessions. Dogs get bored just as humans do. Keep training sessions interesting and exciting. Vary the commands and the locations in which you practice. Give short breaks for play in between lessons. A bored student will never be the best performer in the class.

will be ready to take you at your word and start plotting to destroy the house! Before you collected your puppy, you decided where his own special place would be, and that's where to put him when you first arrive home. Give him a house tour after he has investigated his area and had a nap and a bathroom "pit stop."

It's worth mentioning here that if you've adopted an adult dog that is completely trained to your liking, lucky you! You're off the hook! However, if that dog spent his life up to this point in a

The Bloodhound, properly raised and socialized, can make a focused and willing student.

That's why your puppy is rewarded with small treats along with verbal praise when he responds to you correctly. As the puppy learns to do what you want him to do, the food rewards are gradually eliminated and only the praise remains. If you keep up with the food treats, you could have two problems on your hands—an obese dog and a beggar.

Training begins the minute your puppy steps through the doorway of your home, so don't make the mistake of putting the puppy on the floor and telling him by your actions, "Go for it! Run wild!" Even if this is your first puppy, you must act as if you know what you're doing: be the boss. An uncertain pup may be terrified to move, while a bold one

kennel, or even in a good home but without any real training, be prepared to tackle the job ahead. A dog three years of age or older with no previous training cannot be blamed for not knowing what he was never taught. While the dog is trying to understand and learn your rules, at the same time he has to unlearn many of his previously self-taught habits and general view of the world.

Working with a professional trainer will speed up your progress with an adopted adult dog. You'll need patience, too. Some new rules may be close to impossible for the dog to accept. After all, he's been successful so far by doing everything his way! (Patience again.) He may agree with your instruction for a few days and then slip back into his old ways, so you must be just as consistent and understanding in your teaching as you would be with a puppy. (More patience needed yet again!) Your dog has to learn to pay attention to your voice, your family, the daily routine, new smells, new sounds and, in some cases, even a new climate.

One of the most important things to find out about a newly adopted adult dog is his reaction to children (yours and others), strangers and your friends, and how he acts upon meeting other dogs. If he was not socialized with dogs as a puppy, this could be a

TIDY BOY
Clean by nature, dogs do not like to soil their dens, which in effect are their crates or sleeping quarters. Unless not feeling well, dogs will not defecate or urinate in their crates. Crate training capitalizes on the dog's natural desire to keep his den clean. Be conscientious about giving the puppy as many opportunities to relieve himself outdoors as possible. Reward the puppy for correct behavior. Praise him and pat his head whenever he "goes" in the correct location. Even the tidiest of puppies can have potty accidents, so be patient and dedicate more energy to helping your puppy achieve a clean lifestyle.

major problem. This does not mean that he's a "bad" dog, a vicious dog or an aggressive dog; rather, it means that he has no idea how to read another dog's body language. There's no way for him to tell if the other dog is a friend or foe. Survival instinct takes over, telling him to attack first and ask questions later. This definitely calls for professional help and, even then, may not be a behavior that can be corrected 100% reliably (or even at all). If you have a puppy, this is why it is so very important to introduce your young puppy properly to other puppies and "dog-friendly" adult dogs.

HOUSE-TRAINING

Dogs are tactile-oriented when it comes to house-training. In other words, they respond to the surface on which they are given approval to eliminate. The choice is yours (the dog's version is in parentheses): The lawn (including the neighbors' lawns)? A bare patch of earth under a tree (where people like to sit and relax in the summertime)? Concrete steps or patio (all sidewalks, garage and basement floors)? The curbside (watch out for cars)? A small area of crushed stone in a corner of the yard (mine!)? The latter is the best choice if you can manage it because it will remain strictly for the dog's use and is easy to keep clean.

You can start out with paper-training indoors and switch over to an outdoor surface as the puppy matures and gains control over his need to eliminate. For the nay-sayers, don't worry—this won't mean that the dog will soil on every piece of newspaper lying around the house. You are training him to go outside, remember? Starting out by paper-training often is the only choice for a city dog.

WHEN YOUR PUPPY'S "GOT TO GO"

Your puppy's need to relieve himself is seemingly non-stop, but signs of improvement will be seen each week. From 8 to 10 weeks old, the puppy will have to be

THE RIGHT START
The best advice for a potential dog owner is to start with the very best puppy that money can buy. Don't shop around for a bargain in the newspaper. You're buying a companion, not a used Buick or a second-hand Maytag. The purchase price of the dog represents the most important part of the investment, but this is indeed a very small sum compared to the expenses of maintaining the dog in good health. If you purchase a well-bred, healthy and sound puppy, you will be starting right. An unhealthy puppy can cost you thousands of dollars in unnecessary veterinary expenses and, possibly, a fortune in heartbreak as well.

CANINE DEVELOPMENT SCHEDULE

It is important to understand how and at what age a puppy develops into adulthood. If you are a puppy owner, consult the following Canine Development Schedule to determine the stage of development your puppy is currently experiencing. This knowledge will help you as you work with the puppy in the weeks and months ahead.

Period	Age	Characteristics
FIRST TO THIRD	BIRTH TO SEVEN WEEKS	Puppy needs food, sleep and warmth, and responds to simple and gentle touching. Needs mother for security and disciplining. Needs littermates for learning and interacting with other dogs. Pup learns to function within a pack and learns pack order of dominance. Begin socializing pup with adults and children for short periods. Pup begins to become aware of his environment.
FOURTH	EIGHT TO TWELVE WEEKS	Brain is fully developed. Pup needs socializing with outside world. Remove from mother and littermates. Needs to change from canine pack to human pack. Human dominance necessary. Fear period occurs between 8 and 12 weeks. Avoid fright and pain.
FIFTH	THIRTEEN TO SIXTEEN WEEKS	Training and formal obedience should begin. Less association with other dogs, more with people, places, situations. Period will pass easily if you remember this is pup's change-to-adolescence time. Be firm and fair. Flight instinct prominent. Permissiveness and over-disciplining can do permanent damage. Praise for good behavior.
JUVENILE	FOUR TO EIGHT MONTHS	Another fear period about 7 to 8 months of age. It passes quickly, but be cautious of fright and pain. Sexual maturity reached. Dominant traits established. Dog should understand sit, down, come and stay by now.

NOTE: THESE ARE APPROXIMATE TIME FRAMES. ALLOW FOR INDIVIDUAL DIFFERENCES IN PUPPIES.

taken outside every time he wakes up, about 10–15 minutes after every meal and after every period of play—all day long, from first thing in the morning until his bedtime! That's a total of ten or more trips per day to teach the puppy where it's okay to relieve himself. With that schedule in mind, you can see that house-training a young puppy is not a part-time job. It requires someone to be home all day.

If that seems overwhelming or impossible, do a little planning. For example, plan to pick up your puppy at the start of a vacation period. If you can't get home in the middle of the day, plan to hire a dog-sitter or ask a neighbor to come over to take the pup outside, feed him his lunch and then take him out again about ten or so minutes after he's eaten. Also make arrangements with that or another person to be your "emergency" contact if you have to stay late on the job. Remind yourself—repeatedly—that this hectic schedule improves as the puppy gets older.

HOME WITHIN A HOME

Your puppy needs to be confined to one secure, puppy-proof area when no one is able to watch his every move. Generally, the kitchen is the place of choice because the floor is washable. Likewise, it's a busy family area that will accustom the pup to a

EXTRA! EXTRA!
The headlines read: "Puppy Piddles Here!" Breeders commonly use newspapers to line their whelping pens, thus puppies learn to associate newspapers with relieving themselves. Do not use newspapers to line your pup's crate, as this will signal to your puppy that it is OK to urinate in his crate. If you choose to paper-train your puppy, you will layer newspapers on a section of the floor near the door he uses to go outside. You should encourage the puppy to use the papers to relieve himself, and bring him there whenever you see him getting ready to go. Little by little, you will reduce the size of the newspaper-covered area so that the puppy will learn to relieve himself "on the other side of the door."

variety of noises, everything from pots and pans to the telephone, blender and dishwasher. He will also be enchanted by the smell of your cooking (and will never be critical when you burn something). An exercise pen (also

called an "ex-pen," a puppy
version of a playpen) within the
room of choice is an excellent
means of confinement for a young
pup. He can see out and has a
certain amount of space in which
to run about, but he is safe from
dangerous things like electrical
cords, heating units, trash baskets
or open kitchen-supply cabinets.
Place the pen where the puppy
will not get a blast of heat or air
conditioning.

In the pen, you can put a few
toys, his bed (which can be his
crate if the dimensions of pen and
crate are compatible) and a few
layers of newspaper in one small
corner, just in case. A water bowl
can be hung at a convenient
height on the side of the ex-pen so
it won't become a splashing pool
for an innovative puppy. His food
dish can go on the floor, next to
the water bowl.

Crates are something that pet
owners are at last getting used to
for their dogs. Wild or domestic
canines have always preferred to
sleep in den-like safe spots, and
that is exactly what the crate
provides. How often have you
seen adult dogs that choose to
sleep under a table or chair even
though they have full run of the
house? It's the den connection.

The crate can be solid
(fiberglass) with ventilation on the
upper sides and a wire-grate door
that locks securely, or it can be of
open wire construction with a

SOMEBODY TO BLAME
House-training a puppy can be
frustrating for the puppy and the
owner alike. The puppy does not
instinctively understand the
difference between defecating on the
pavement outside and piddling on the
ceramic tile in the kitchen. He is
confused and frightened by his
human's exuberant reactions to his
natural urges. The owner, arguably the
more intelligent of the duo, is also
frustrated that he cannot convince his
puppy to obey his commands and
instructions.

In frustration, the owner may
struggle with the temptation to
discipline the puppy, scold him or
even strike the puppy on the rear end.
Shouting and smacking the puppy may
make you feel better, but it will defeat
your purpose in gaining your puppy's
trust and respect. Don't blame your
nine-week-old puppy. Blame yourself
for not being 100% consistent in the
puppy's lessons and routine. The
lesson here is simple: try harder and
your puppy will succeed, too.

solid floor. Your puppy will go
along with whichever one you
prefer. The open wire crate,
however, should be covered at
night to give the snug feeling of a
den. A blanket or towel over the
top will be fine.

The crate should be big
enough for the adult dog to stand
up and turn around in, even
though he may spend much of his

time curled up in the back part of it. There are movable barriers that fit inside dog crates to provide the right amount of space for small puppies that grow into large dogs. Never afford a young puppy too much space, thinking that you're being kind and generous. He'll just sleep at one end of the crate and soil in the other end! While you should purchase only one crate, one that will accommodate your pup when grown, you will need to make use of the partitions so that the pup has a comfortable area without enough extra space to use as a toilet. A dog does not like to soil where he sleeps, so you are teaching him to "hold it" until it's time for a trip outside. You may want an extra crate to keep in the car for safe traveling.

In your "happy" voice, use the word "Crate" every time you put the pup in his den. If he's new to a crate, toss in a small biscuit for him to chase the first few times. At night, after he's been outside, he should sleep in his crate. The crate may be kept in his designated area at night or, if you want to be sure to hear those wake-up yips in the morning, put the crate in a corner of your bedroom. However, don't make any response whatsoever to whining or crying. If he's completely ignored, he'll settle down and get to sleep.

Good bedding for a young puppy is an old folded bath towel or an old blanket, something that is easily washable and disposable if necessary ("accidents" will happen!). Never put newspaper in the puppy's crate. Those old ideas of adding a clock to replace his mother's heartbeat, or a hot-water bottle to replace her warmth, are just that—old ideas. The clock could drive the puppy nuts, and the hot-water bottle could end up as a very soggy waterbed! An extremely good breeder would have introduced your puppy to the crate by letting two pups sleep together for a couple of nights, followed by several nights alone. How thankful you will be if you found that breeder!

Safe toys in the pup's crate or area will keep him occupied, but

Don't expect too much of your Bloodhound puppy all at once. Patience pays off.

monitor their condition closely. Discard any toys that show signs of being chewed to bits. Squeaky parts, bits of stuffing or plastic or any other small pieces can cause intestinal blockage or possibly choking if swallowed.

PROGRESSING WITH POTTY-TRAINING

After you've taken your puppy out and he has relieved himself in the area you've selected, he can have some free time with the family as long as there is someone responsible for watching him. That doesn't mean just someone in the same room who is watching TV or busy on the computer, but one person who is doing nothing other than keeping an eye on the pup, playing with him on the floor and helping him understand his position in the pack.

This first taste of freedom will let you begin to set the house rules. If you don't want the dog on the furniture, now is the time to prevent his first attempts to jump up onto the couch. The word to use in this case is "Off," not "Down." "Down" is the word you will use to teach the down position, which is something entirely different.

Most corrections at this stage come in the form of simply distracting the puppy. Instead of telling him "No" for "Don't chew the carpet," distract the chomping puppy with a toy and he'll forget about the carpet.

As you are playing with the pup, do not forget to watch him closely and pay attention to his body language. Whenever you see him begin to circle or sniff, take the puppy outside to relieve himself. If you are paper-training, put him back in his confined area on the newspapers. In either case, praise him as he eliminates, while he actually is in the act of relieving himself. Three seconds after he has finished is too late! You'll be praising him for running toward you, or picking up a toy or whatever he may be doing at that moment, and that's not what you want to be praising him for. Timing is a vital tool in all dog training. Use it!

Remove soiled newspapers immediately and replace them with clean ones. You may want to take a small piece of soiled paper and place it in the middle of the new clean papers, as the scent will attract him to that spot when it's time to go again. That scent attraction is why it's so important to clean up any messes made in the house with a product specially made to eliminate the odor of dog urine and droppings. Regular household cleansers won't do the trick. Pet shops sell the best pet deodorizers. Invest in the largest container you can find.

Scent attraction eventually will lead your pup to his chosen spot outdoors, too; this is the

DAILY SCHEDULE

How many relief trips does your puppy need per day? A puppy up to the age of 14 weeks will need to go outside about 8 to 12 times per day! You will have to take the pup out any time he starts sniffing around the floor or turning in small circles, as well as after naps, meals, games and lessons or whenever he's released from his crate. Once the puppy is 14 to 22 weeks of age, he will only require 6 to 8 relief trips. At the ages of 22 to 32 weeks, the puppy will require about 5 to 7 trips. Adult dogs typically require 4 relief trips per day, in the morning, afternoon, evening and late at night.

basis of outdoor training. When you take your puppy outside to relieve himself, use a one-word command such as "Outside" or "Go-potty" (that's one word to the puppy!) as you pick him up and attach his leash. Then put him down in his area. If he is too big for you to carry, snap the leash on quickly and lead him to his spot. Now comes the hard part—hard for you, that is. Just stand there until he urinates and defecates. Move him a few feet in one direction or another if he's just sitting there looking at you, but remember that this is neither playtime nor time for a walk. This is strictly a business trip! Then, as he circles and squats (remember

your timing!), give him a quiet "Good dog" as praise. If you start to jump for joy, ecstatic over his performance, he'll do one of two things: either he will stop mid-stream, as it were, or he'll do it again for you—in the house—and expect you to be just as delighted!

Give him five minutes or so and, if he doesn't go in that time, take him back indoors to his confined area and try again in another ten minutes, or immediately if you see him sniffing and circling. By careful observation, you'll soon work out a successful schedule.

Accidents, by the way, are just that—accidents. Clean them up quickly and thoroughly, without comment, after the puppy has been taken outside to finish his business and then put back in his area or crate. If you witness an accident in progress, say "No!" in a stern voice and get the pup outdoors immediately. No punishment is needed. You and your puppy are just learning each other's language and sometimes it's easy to miss a puppy's message. Chalk it up to experience and watch more closely from now on.

KEEPING THE PACK ORDERLY
Discipline is a form of training that brings order to life. For example, military discipline is what allows the soldiers in an army to work as one. Discipline is

a form of teaching and, in dogs, is the basis of how the successful pack operates. Each member knows his place in the pack and all respect the leader, or Alpha dog. It is essential for your puppy that you establish this type of relationship, with you as the Alpha, or leader. It is a form of social coexistence that all canines recognize and accept. Discipline, therefore, is never to be confused with punishment. When you teach your puppy how you want him to behave, and he behaves properly and you praise him for it, you are disciplining him with a form of positive reinforcement.

For a dog, rewards come in the form of praise, a smile, a cheerful tone of voice, a few friendly pats or a rub of the ears.

Although Bloodhounds don't thrive on obedience lessons, they can be attentive students if properly encouraged.

Rewards are also small food treats. Obviously, that does not mean bits of regular dog food. Rather, treats are very small bits of special things like cheese or pieces of soft dog treats. The idea is to reward the dog with something very small that he can taste and swallow, providing instant positive reinforcement. If he has to take time to chew the treat, by the time he is finished, he will have forgotten what he did to earn it!

Your puppy should never be physically punished. The displeasure shown on your face and in your voice is sufficient to signal to the pup that he has done something wrong. He wants to please everyone higher up on the social ladder, especially his leader, so a scowl and harsh voice will take care of the error. Growling out the word "Shame!" when the pup is caught in the act of doing something wrong is better than the repetitive "No." Some dogs hear "No" so often that they begin to think it's their name! By the way, do not use the dog's name when you're correcting him. His name is reserved to get his attention for something pleasant about to take place.

There are punishments that have nothing to do with you. For example, your dog may think that chasing cats is one reason for his existence. You can try to stop it as much as you like without success because it's such fun for the dog. But one good hissing, spitting, swipe of a cat's claws across the dog's nose will put an end to the game forever. Only intervene when you're dog's eyeball is seriously at risk. Cat scratches can cause permanent damage to an innocent but annoying puppy.

PUPPY KINDERGARTEN

COLLAR AND LEASH
Before you begin your puppy's education, he must be used to his collar and leash. Choose a collar for your puppy that is secure, but not heavy or bulky. He won't enjoy training if he's uncomfortable. A flat buckle collar is fine for everyday wear and for initial puppy training. For older dogs, there are several types of training collars such as the martingale, which is a double loop that tightens slightly around the neck, or the head collar, which is similar to a horse's halter. Do not use a chain choke collar unless you have been specifically shown how to put it on and how to use it, especially with the Bloodhound's heavy skin folds.

A lightweight, 6-foot woven cotton or nylon training leash is preferred by most trainers because it is easy to fold up in your hand and comfortable to hold because there is a certain amount of give to it. There are lessons where the dog will start off six feet away

Never underestimate the power of a bribe—in canine terminology, that's a food treat. Most Bloodhounds are motivated by an enticing morsel and will quickly learn to obey a command to get a tidbit.

from you at the end of the leash. The leash used to take the puppy outside to relieve himself is shorter because you don't want him to roam away from his area. The shorter leash will also be the one to use when you walk the puppy for the same reason.

If you've been fortunate enough to enroll in a Kindergarten Puppy Training class, suggestions will be made as to the best collar and leash for your young puppy. We say "fortunate" because your puppy will be in a class with puppies in his age range (up to five months old) of all breeds and sizes. It's the perfect way for him to learn the right way (and the wrong way) to interact with other dogs as well as their people. You cannot teach your puppy how to interpret another dog's sign language. For a first-time puppy owner, these socialization classes are invaluable. For experienced dog owners, they are a real boon to further training.

ATTENTION

You've been using the dog's name since the minute you collected him from the breeder, so you should be able to get his attention by saying his name—with a big smile and in an excited tone of voice. His response will be the puppy equivalent of "Here I am! What are we going to do?" Your immediate response (if you haven't guessed by now) is "Good dog." Rewarding him at the moment he pays attention to you teaches him the proper way to respond when he hears his name.

Teaching the Bloodhound to sit is an excellent place to start the training sessions. Most dogs respond to the sit command quite readily, especially if a food treat is involved.

EXERCISES FOR A BASIC CANINE EDUCATION

THE SIT EXERCISE

There are several ways to teach the puppy to sit. The first one is to catch him whenever he is about to sit and, as his backside nears the floor, say "Sit, good dog!" That's positive reinforcement and, if your timing is sharp, he will learn that what he's doing at that second is connected to your saying "Sit" and that you think he's clever for doing it!

Another method is to start with the puppy on his leash in front of you. Show him a treat in the palm of your right hand. Bring your hand up under his nose and, almost in slow motion, move your hand up and back so his nose goes up in the air and his head tilts back as he follows the treat in your hand. At that point, he will have to either sit or fall over, so as his back legs buckle under, say "Sit, good dog," and then give him the treat and lots of praise. You may have to begin with your hand lightly running up his chest, actually lifting his chin up until he sits. Some (usually older) dogs require gentle pressure on their hindquarters with the left hand, in which case the dog should be on your left side. Puppies generally do not appreciate physical dominance of this nature.

After a few times, you should

be able to show the dog a treat in the open palm of your hand, raise your hand waist-high as you say "Sit" and have him sit. Once again, you have taught him two things at the same time. The verbal command and the motion of the hand are both signals for the sit. Your puppy is watching you almost more than he is listening to you, so what you do is just as important as what you say.

Don't save any of these drills only for training sessions. Use them as much as possible at odd times during a normal day. The dog should always sit before being given his food dish. He should sit to let you go through a doorway first, when the doorbell rings or when you stop to speak to someone on the street.

THE DOWN EXERCISE

Before beginning to teach the down command, you must consider how the dog feels about this exercise. To him, "down" is a submissive position. Being flat on the floor with you standing over him is not his idea of fun. It's up to you to let him know that, while it may not be fun, the reward of your approval is worth his effort.

Start with the puppy on your left side in a sit position. Hold the leash right above his collar in your left hand. Have an extra-special treat, such as a small piece of cooked chicken or hot dog, in your right hand. Place it at the

end of the pup's nose and steadily move your hand down and forward along the ground. Hold the leash to prevent a sudden lunge for the food. As the puppy goes into the down position, say "Down" very gently.

The difficulty with this exercise is twofold: it's both the submissive aspect and the fact that most people say the word "Down" as if they were a drill sergeant in charge of recruits! So issue the command sweetly, give him the treat and have the pup maintain the down position for several seconds. If he tries to get up immediately, place your hands on his shoulders and press down gently, giving him a very quiet "Good dog." As you progress with this lesson, increase the "down time" until he will hold it until you say "Okay" (his cue for release). Practice this one in the house at various times throughout the day.

By increasing the length of time during which the dog must maintain the down position,

Be reassuring and gentle when teaching your Bloodhound the down position. It's okay to get down on his level to teach this exercise.

you'll find many uses for it. For example, he can lie at your feet in the vet's office or anywhere that both of you have to wait, when you are on the phone, while the family is eating and so forth. If you progress to training for competitive obedience, he'll already be all set for the exercise called the "long down."

THE STAY EXERCISES

To teach the sit/stay, have the dog sit on your left side. Hold the leash at waist level in your left hand and let the dog know that you have a treat in your closed right hand. Step forward on your right foot as you say "Stay." Immediately turn and stand directly in front of the dog,

Reinforce the stay command with the hand signal. Practice the stay in both the sit and down positions.

keeping your right hand up high so he'll keep his eye on the treat hand and maintain the sit position for a count of five. Return to your original position and offer the reward.

Increase the length of the sit/stay each time until the dog can hold it for at least 30 seconds without moving. After about a week of success, move out on your right foot and take two steps before turning to face the dog. Give the "Stay" hand signal (left palm back toward the dog's head) as you leave. He gets the treat when you return and he holds the sit/stay. Increase the distance that you walk away from him before turning until you reach the length of your training leash. But don't rush it! Go back to the beginning if he moves before he should. No matter what the lesson, never be upset by having to back up for a few days. The repetition and practice are what will make your dog reliable in these commands. It won't do any good to move on to something more difficult if the command is not mastered at the easier levels. Above all, even if you do get frustrated, never let your puppy know! Always keep a positive, upbeat attitude during training, which will transmit to your dog for positive results.

The down/stay is taught in the same way once the dog is completely reliable and steady with the down command. Again, don't rush it. With the dog in the down position on your left side, step out on your right foot as you say "Stay." Return by walking around in back of the dog and into your original position. While you are training, it's okay to murmur something like "Hold on" to encourage him to stay put. When the dog will stay without moving when you are at a distance of 3 or 4 feet, begin to increase the length of time before you return. Be sure he holds the down on your return until you say "Okay." At that point, he gets his treat—just so he'll remember for next time that it's not over until it's over.

THE COME EXERCISE

No command is more important to the safety of your dog than "come." It is what you should say every single time you see the puppy running toward you: "Binky, come! Good dog." During playtime, run a few feet away from the puppy, turn and tell him to "come" as he is already running to you. You can go so far as to teach your puppy two things at once if you squat down and hold out your arms. As the pup gets close to you and you're saying "Good dog," bring your right arm in about waist-high. Now he's also learning the hand signal, an excellent device should you be on the phone when you need to get him to come to you!

You'll also both be one step ahead when you enter obedience classes.

Puppies, like children, have notoriously short attention spans, so don't overdo it with any of the training. Keep each lesson short. Break it up with a quick run around the yard or a ball toss, repeat the lesson and quit as soon as the pup gets it right. That way, you will always end with a "Good dog."

When the puppy responds to your well-timed "Come," try it with the puppy on the training leash. This time, catch him off guard, while he's sniffing a leaf or watching a bird: "Binky, come!" You may have to pause for a split second after his name to be sure you have his attention. If the puppy shows any sign of confusion, give the leash a mild jerk and take a couple of steps backward. Do not repeat the command. In this case, as he reaches you, you should say "Good come!"

Include the children in your "Where are you?" lessons. Your Bloodhound will enjoy a tussle with the members of his family pack.

I WILL FOLLOW YOU

Obedience isn't just a classroom activity. In your home, you have many great opportunities to teach your dog polite manners. Allowing your pet on the bed or furniture elevates him to your level, which is not a good idea (the word is "Off!"). Use the "umbilical cord" method, keeping your dog on lead so he has to go with you wherever you go. You sit, he sits. You walk, he heels. You stop, he sit-stays. Everywhere you go, he's with you, but you go first!

if you are angry or intend to correct him for some misbehavior. When correcting the pup, you go to him. Your dog must always connect "come" with something pleasant and with your approval; then you can rely on his response. Life isn't perfect and neither are puppies. A time will come, often around 10 months of age, when he'll become "selectively deaf" or choose to "forget" his name. He may respond by wagging his tail (and even seeming to smile at you) with a look that says "Make me!" Laugh, throw his favorite toy and skip the lesson you had planned. Pups will be pups!

THE HEEL EXERCISE

The second most important command to teach, after the come, is the heel. When you are walking your growing puppy, you need to be in control. Besides, it looks terrible to be pulled and yanked down the street, and it's not much fun either! Your eight-to ten-week old puppy will probably follow you everywhere, but that's his natural instinct, not your control over the situation. However, any time he does follow you, you can say "Heel" and be ahead of the game, as he will learn to associate this command with the action of following you before you even begin teaching him to heel.

There is a very precise, almost military, procedure for teaching your dog to heel. As with all

That's the number-one rule of training. Each command word is given just once. Anything more is nagging. You'll also notice that all commands are one word only. Even when they are actually two words, you say them as one.

Never call the dog to come to you—with or without his name—

obedience training, begin with the dog on your left side. He will be in a very nice sit and you will have the training leash across your chest. Hold the loop and folded leash in your right hand. Pick up the slack leash above the dog in your left hand and hold it loosely at your side. Step out on your left foot as you say "Heel." If the puppy does not move, give a gentle tug or pat your left leg to get him started. If he surges ahead of you, stop and pull him back gently until he is at your side. Tell him to sit and begin again.

Walk a few steps and stop while the puppy is correctly beside you. Tell him to sit and give mild verbal praise. (More enthusiastic praise will encourage him to think the lesson is over.) Repeat the lesson, only increasing the number of steps you take as long as the dog is heeling nicely beside you. When you end the lesson, have him hold the sit, then give him the "Okay" to let him know that this is the end of the lesson. Praise him so that he knows he did a good job.

The cure for excessive pulling (a common problem) is to stop when the dog is no more than 2 or 3 feet ahead of you. Guide him back into position and begin again. With a really determined puller, try switching to a head collar. This will automatically turn the pup's head toward you so you can bring him back easily to the heel position. Give quiet, reassuring praise every time the leash goes slack and he's staying with you.

Staying and heeling can take a lot out of a dog, so provide playtime and free-running exercise when the lessons are over to shake off the stress. You don't want him to associate training with all work and no fun.

TAPERING OFF TIDBITS
Your dog has been watching you—and the hand that treats—throughout all of his lessons, and now it's time to break the treat habit. Begin by giving him treats at the end of each lesson only. Then start to give a treat after the end of only some of the lessons. At the end of every lesson, as well

Before you start the heel lessons, make sure your puppy is comfortable walking on a leash.

and other handlers can help you to find the most efficient way of teaching your dog a command or exercise. It's often easier to learn from other people's mistakes than your own. You will also learn all of the requirements for competitive obedience trials, in which you can earn titles and go on to advanced jumping and retrieving exercises, which are fun for many dogs. Obedience classes build the foundation needed for many other canine activities (in which we humans are allowed to participate, too!).

A well-trained pack of Bloodhounds does what comes naturally, hunting in organized events in the company of horses and horsemen.

as during the lessons, be consistent with the praise. Your pup now doesn't know if he'll get a treat or not, but he should keep performing well just in case! Finally, you will stop giving treat rewards entirely. Save them for something brand-new that you want to teach him. Keep up the praise and you'll always have a "good dog."

OBEDIENCE CLASSES

The advantages of an obedience class are that your dog will have to learn amid the distractions of other people and dogs and that your mistakes will be quickly corrected by the trainer. Teaching your dog along with a qualified instructor and other handlers who may have more dog experience than you is a further plus of the class environment. The instructor

TRAINING FOR OTHER ACTIVITIES

Once your dog has basic obedience under his collar, and is 12 months of age, you can enter the world of agility training. Dogs think agility is pure fun, like being turned loose in an amusement park full of obstacles! In addition to agility, there are hunting activities for sporting dogs, lure-coursing events for sighthounds, go-to-ground events for terriers, racing for the Nordic sled dogs, herding trials for the shepherd breeds and tracking, which is open to all "nosey" dogs (which would include all dogs!). For those who like to volunteer, there is the wonderful feeling of owning a Therapy Dog and visiting hospices, nursing homes and veterans' homes to bring smiles, comfort and companionship to those who live there.

Around the house, your dog can be taught to do some simple chores. You might teach him to carry a basket of household items or to fetch the morning newspaper. The kids can teach the dog all kinds of tricks, from playing hide-and-seek to balancing a biscuit on his nose. A family dog is what rounds out the family. Everything he does beyond sitting in your lap or gazing lovingly at you represents the bonus of owning a dog. Not ideal candidates for agility trials, obedience shows or working trials, Bloodhounds are best suited to man-trailing, an activity that serves their human owners

and companions. They do not excel in formal obedience competition, nor are they well suited to any type of hunting today, except in organized events. Basic obedience, as a part of proper acceptable behavior, is mandatory to maintain reasonable control over such a large and strong-willed animal.

Bloodhounds excel at swimming and can be trained to enter the water on command. Swimming is the perfect exercise for the breed, and puts no strain on its heavy frame.

MORE PRAISE, LESS FOOD

As you progress with your puppy's lessons, and the puppy is responding well, gradually begin to withhold the treats by alternating the use of treats with times when you offer only verbal praise or a few pats on the dog's side. (Pats on the head are dominant actions and he won't think they are meant to be praise.) Every lesson should end with the puppy's performing the correct action for that session's command. When he gets it right and you withhold the treat, the praise can be as long and lavish as you like. The commands are one word only, but your verbal praise can use as many words as you want...don't skimp on telling your dog he's a good boy!

Tally ho! A hunting event befitting the breed's noble heritage—here's the winning pack with its trophy.

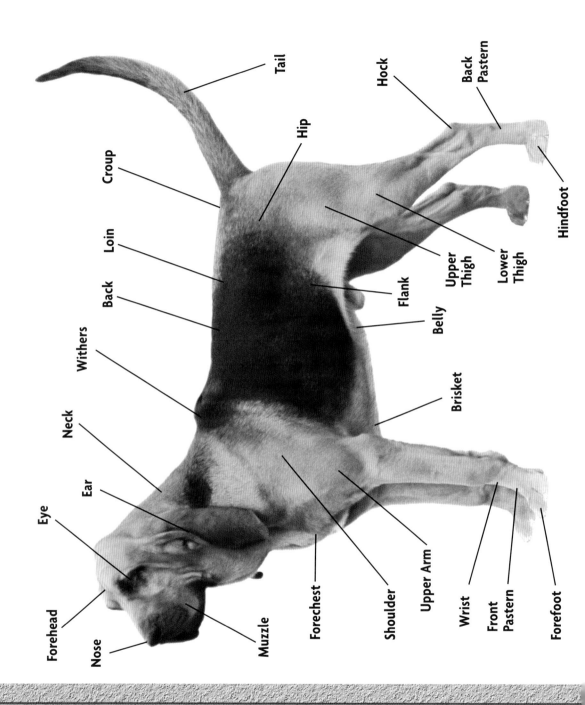

Tail

Hock

Back
Pastern

Hip

Hindfoot

Croup

Upper
Thigh

Lower
Thigh

Loin

Flank

Back

Belly

Withers

Brisket

Neck

Ear

Eye

Forechest

Shoulder

Upper Arm

Wrist

Front
Pastern

Forefoot

Forehead

Nose

Muzzle

PHYSICAL STRUCTURE OF THE BLOODHOUND

BLOODHOUND

BY LOWELL ACKERMAN DVM, DACVD

HEALTHCARE FOR A LIFETIME

When you own a dog, you become his healthcare advocate over his entire lifespan, as well as being the one to shoulder the financial burden of such care. Accordingly, it is worthwhile to focus on prevention rather than treatment, as you and your pet will both be happier.

Of course, the best place to have begun your program of preventative healthcare is with the initial purchase or adoption of your dog. There is no way of guaranteeing that your new furry friend is free of medical problems, but there are some things you can do to improve your odds. You certainly should have done adequate research into your breed of choice and have selected your puppy carefully rather than buying on impulse. Health issues aside, a large number of pet abandonment and relinquishment cases arise from a mismatch between pet needs and owner expectations. This is entirely preventable with appropriate planning and finding a good breeder.

Regarding healthcare issues specifically, it is very difficult to make blanket statements about where to acquire a problem-free

pet, but, again, a reputable breeder is your best bet. In an ideal situation, you have the opportunity to see both parents, get references from other owners of the breeder's pups and see genetic-testing documentation for several generations of the litter's ancestors. At the very least, you must thoroughly investigate your breed of interest and the problems inherent in that breed, as well as the genetic testing available to screen for those problems. Genetic testing offers some important benefits, but testing is only available for a few disorders in a relatively small number of breeds and is not available for some of the most common genetic diseases, such as hip dysplasia, cataracts, epilepsy, cardiomyopathy, etc. This area of research is indeed exciting and increasingly important, and advances will continue to be made each year. In fact, recent research has shown that there is an equivalent dog gene for 75% of known human genes, so research done in either species is likely to benefit the other.

We've also discussed that evaluating your chosen pup's behavioral nature and that of his immediate family members is an

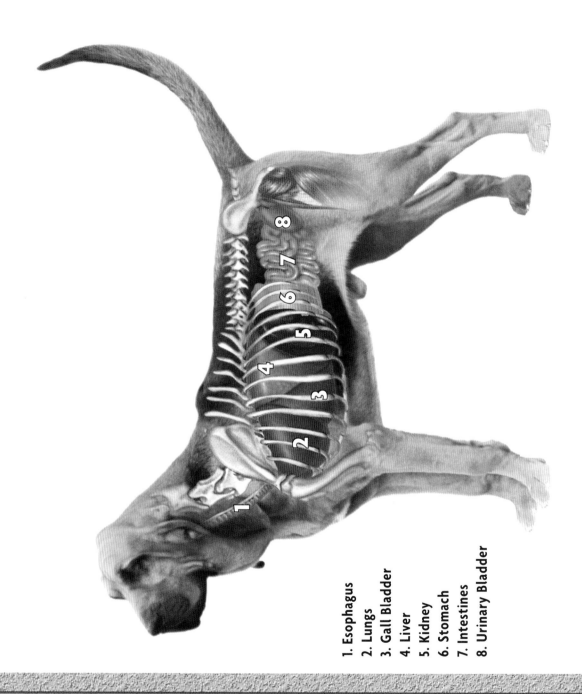

1. Esophagus
2. Lungs
3. Gall Bladder
4. Liver
5. Kidney
6. Stomach
7. Intestines
8. Urinary Bladder

INTERNAL ORGANS OF THE BLOODHOUND

YOUR DOG NEEDS TO VISIT THE VET IF:
- He has ingested a toxin such as antifreeze or a toxic plant; in these cases, administer first aid and call the vet right away
- His teeth are discolored, loose, missing or he has sores and/or other signs of infection or abnormality in the mouth
- He has been vomiting, has had diarrhea or has been constipated for over 24 hours, or immediately if you notice blood
- He has refused food for over 24 hours
- His weight, eating habits, water intake and/or toilet habits have noticeably increased or decreased; have noticed weight gain or weight loss
- He shows symptoms of bloat, , which require immediate attention
- He is salivating excessively
- He has a lump in his throat
- He has a lumps or bumps anywhere on the body
- He is very lethargic
- He appears to be in pain or otherwise have trouble chewing or swallowing
- His skin loses elasticity.

Of course, there will be other instances in which a visit to the vet is necessary; these are just some of the signs that could be indicative of serious problems that need to be caught as early on as possible.

important part of the selection process that cannot be underestimated or underemphasized. It is sometimes difficult to evaluate temperament in puppies because certain behavioral tendencies, such as some forms of aggression, may not be immediately evident. More dogs are euthanized each year for behavioral reasons than for all medical conditions combined, so it is critical to take temperament issues seriously. Start with a well-balanced, friendly companion and put the time and effort into proper socialization, and you will both be rewarded with a lifelong valued relationship.

With a pup from healthy, sound stock, you become responsible for helping your veterinarian keep your pet healthy. Some crucial things happen before you even bring your puppy home. Parasite control typically begins at two weeks of age and vaccinations typically begin at six to eight weeks of age. A pre-pubertal evaluation is typically scheduled for about six months of age. At this time, a dental evaluation is done (since the adult teeth are now in), heartworm prevention is started and neutering or spaying is most commonly done.

It is critical to commence regular dental care at home if you have not already done so. It may not sound so important, but most dogs have active periodontal disease by four years of age if they

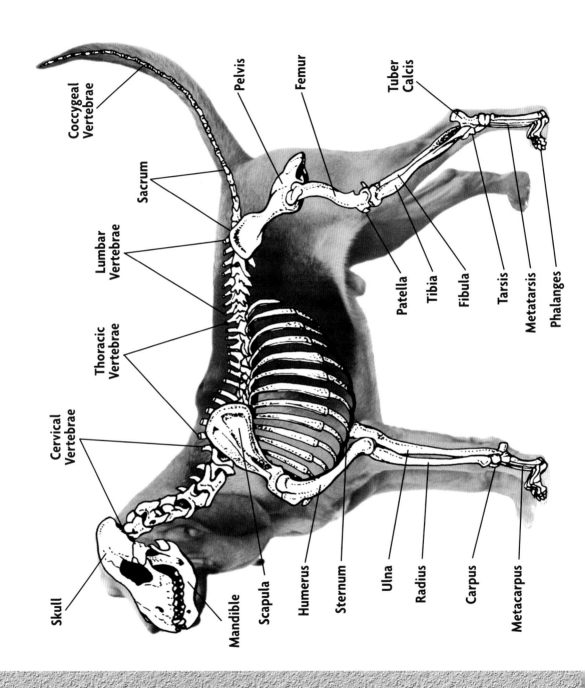

Coccygeal Vertebrae

Pelvis

Femur

Tuber Calcis

Sacrum

Lumbar Vertebrae

Patella

Tibia

Fibula

Tarsis

Metatarsis

Phalanges

Thoracic Vertebrae

Cervical Vertebrae

Skull

Mandible

Scapula

Humerus

Sternum

Ulna

Radius

Carpus

Metacarpus

SKELETAL STRUCTURE OF THE BLOODHOUND

don't have their teeth cleaned regularly at home, not just at their veterinary exams. Dental problems lead to more than just bad "doggie breath": gum disease can have very serious medical consequences. If you start brushing your dog's teeth and using antiseptic rinses from a young age, your dog will be accustomed to it and will not resist. The results will be healthy dentition, which your pet will need to enjoy a long, healthy life.

Most dogs are considered adults at a year of age, although some larger breeds still have some filling out to do up to about two or so years old. Each breed has different healthcare requirements, so work with your veterinarian to determine what will be needed and what your role should be. This doctor-client relationship is important, because as vaccination guidelines change, there may not be an annual "vaccine visit" scheduled. You must make sure that you see your veterinarian at least annually, even if no vaccines are due, because this is the best opportunity to coordinate health-care activities and to make sure that no medical issues creep by unaddressed.

When your pet reaches three-quarters of his anticipated lifespan, he is considered a "senior" and likely requires some special care. In general, if you've been taking great care of your canine companion throughout his formative and adult years, the transition to senior status should be a smooth one. Age is not a disease, and as long as everything is functioning as it should, there is no reason why most of late adulthood should not be rewarding for both you and your pet. This is especially true if you have tended to the details, such as regular veterinary visits, proper dental care, excellent nutrition and management of bone and joint issues.

At this stage in your dog's life, your veterinarian may want to schedule visits twice yearly, instead of once, to run some labora-tory screenings, electrocardiograms and the like, and to change the diet to something more digestible. Catching problems early is the best way to manage them effectively. Treating the early stages of heart disease is so much easier than trying to intervene when there is more significant damage to the heart muscle. Similarly, managing the beginning of kidney problems is fairly routine if there is no signif-icant kidney damage. Other problems, like cognitive dysfunc-tion (similar to senility and Alzheimer's disease), cancer, diabetes and arthritis, are more common in older dogs, but all can be treated to help the dog live as many happy, comfortable years as possible. Just as in people, medical management is more effective (and less expensive) when you catch things early.

KNOW WHEN TO POSTPONE A VACCINATION

While the visit to the vet is costly, it is never advisable to update a vaccination when visiting with a sick or pregnant dog. Vaccinations should be avoided for all elderly dogs. If your dog is showing the signs of any illness or any medical condition, no matter how serious or mild, including skin irritations, do not vaccinate. Likewise, a lame dog should never be vaccinated; any dog undergoing surgery or on any immunosuppressant drugs should not be vaccinated until fully recovered.

SELECTING A VETERINARIAN

There is probably no more important decision that you will make regarding your pet's health-care than the selection of his doctor. Your pet's veterinarian will be a pediatrician, family-practice physician and gerontologist, depending on the dog's life stage, and will be the individual who makes recommendations regarding issues such as when specialists need to be consulted, when diagnostic testing and/or therapeutic intervention is needed and when you will need to seek outside emergency and critical-care services. Your vet will act as your advocate and liaison throughout these processes.

Everyone has his own idea about what to look for in a vet, an individual who will play a big role in his dog's (and, of course, his own) life for many years to come. For some, it is the compassionate caregiver with whom they hope to develop a professional relationship to span the lifetime of their dogs and even their future pets. For others, they are seeking a clinician with keen diagnostic and therapeutic insight, who can deliver state-of-the-art healthcare. Still others need a veterinary facility that is open evenings and weekends, or is in close proximity, or provides mobile veterinary services, to accommodate their schedules; these people may not much mind that their dogs might see different veterinarians on each visit. Just as we have different reasons for selecting our own healthcare professionals (e.g., covered by insurance plan, expert in field, convenient location, etc.), we should not expect that there is a one-size-fits-all recommendation for selecting a veterinarian and veterinary practice. The best advice is to be honest in your assessment of what you expect from a veteri-nary practice and to conscien-tiously research the options in your area. You will quickly appreciate that not all veterinary practices are the same and you will be happiest with one that truly meets your needs.

There is another point to be considered in the selection of

veterinary services. Not that long ago, a single veterinarian would attempt to manage all medical and surgical issues as they arose. That was often problematic, because veterinarians are trained in many species and many diseases, and it was just impossible for general veterinary practitioners to be experts in every species, every field and every ailment. However, just as in the human healthcare fields, specialization has allowed general practitioners to concentrate on primary healthcare delivery, especially wellness and the prevention of infectious diseases, and to utilize a network of specialists to assist in the management of conditions that require specific expertise and experience. Thus there are now many types of veterinary specialists, including dermatologists, cardiologists, ophthalmologists, surgeons,

internists, oncologists, neurologists, behaviorists, criticalists and others to help primary-care veterinarians deal with complicated medical challenges. In most cases, specialists see cases referred by primary-care veterinarians, make diagnoses and set up management plans. From there, the animals' ongoing care is returned to their primary-care veterinarians. This important team approach to your pet's medical care needs has provided opportunities for advanced care and an unparalleled level of quality to be delivered.

With all of the opportunities for your pet to receive high-quality veterinary medical care, there is another topic that needs to be addressed at the same time—cost. It's been said that you can have excellent healthcare or inexpensive healthcare, but never both; this is as true in veterinary medicine as it is

Skin problems are common in all breeds, and the Bloodhound is, unfortunately, no exception. If your pup is continually licking at an area, it is wise to have the vet give it a look.

in human medicine. While veterinary costs are a fraction of what the same services cost in the human healthcare arena, it is still difficult to deal with unanticipated medical costs, especially since they can easily creep into hundreds or even thousands of dollars if specialists or emergency services become involved. However, there are ways of managing these risks. The easiest is to buy pet health insurance and realize that its foremost purpose is not to cover routine healthcare visits but rather to serve as an umbrella for those rainy days when your pet needs medical care and you don't want to worry about whether or not you can afford care.

Pet insurance policies are very cost-effective (and very inexpensive by human health insurance standards), but make sure that you buy the policy long before you intend to use it (preferably starting in puppyhood, because coverage will exclude pre-existing conditions) and that you are actually buying an indemnity insurance plan from an insurance company that is regulated by your state or province. Many insurance policy look-alikes are actually discount clubs that are only redeemable at specific locations and for specific services. An indemnity plan covers your pet at almost all veterinary, specialty and emergency practices and is an excellent way to manage your pet's ongoing healthcare needs.

ASK THE VET

Help your vet help you become a well-informed dog owner. Don't be shy about becoming involved in your puppy's veterinary care by asking questions and gaining as much knowledge as you can. For starters, ask what shots your puppy is getting and what diseases they prevent, and discuss with your vet the safest way to vaccinate. Find out what is involved in your dog's annual wellness visits. If you plan to spay or neuter, discuss the best age at which to have this done. Start out on the right "paw" with your puppy's vet and develop good communication with him, as he will care for your dog's health throughout the dog's entire life.

VACCINATIONS AND INFECTIOUS DISEASES

There has never been an easier time to prevent a variety of infectious diseases in your dog, but these advances come with a price—choice. Now, while it may seem that choice is a good thing (and it is), it has never been more difficult for the pet owner (or the veterinarian) to make an informed decision about the best way to protect pets through vaccination.

Years ago, it was just accepted that puppies got a starter series of vaccinations and then annual "boosters" throughout their lives to keep them protected. As more and more vaccines became available, consumers wanted the convenience of having all of that protection in a single injection. The result was "multivalent" vaccines that crammed a lot of protection into a single syringe. The manufacturers' recommendations were to give the vaccines annually, and this was a simple enough protocol to follow. However, as veterinary medicine has become more sophisticated and we have started looking more at healthcare quandaries rather than convenience, it became necessary to reevaluate the situation and deal

with some tough questions. It is important to realize that whether or not to use a particular vaccine depends on the risk of contracting the disease against which it protects, the severity of the disease it if is contracted, the duration of immunity provided by the vaccine, the safety of the product and the needs of the individual animal. In a very general sense, rabies, distemper, hepatitis and parvovirus are considered core vaccine needs, while parainfluenza, *Bordetella bronchiseptica,* leptospirosis, coronavirus and borreliosis (Lyme disease) are considered non-core needs and best reserved for animals that demonstrate reasonable risk of contracting the diseases.

THE GREAT VACCINATION DEBATE

What kinds of questions need to be addressed? When the vet injects multiple organisms at the same time, might some of the components interfere with one another in the development of immunologic protection? We don't have the comprehensive answer to that question, but it does appear that the immune system better handles agents when given individually. Unfortunately, most manufacturers still bundle their vaccine components because that is what most pet owners want, so getting vaccines with single components can sometimes be difficult.

Another question has to do

TAKING YOUR DOG'S TEMPERATURE

It is important to know how to take your dog's temperature at times when you think he may be ill. It's not the most enjoyable task, but it can be done without too much difficulty. It's easier with a helper, preferably someone with whom the dog is friendly, so that one of you can hold the dog while the other inserts the thermometer.

Before inserting the thermometer, coat the end with petroleum jelly. Insert the thermometer slowly and gently into the dog's rectum about one inch. Wait for the reading, about two minutes. Be sure to remove the thermometer carefully and clean it thoroughly after each use.

A dog's normal body temperature is between 100.5 and 102.5 degrees F. Immediate veterinary attention is required if the dog's temperature is below 99 or above 104 degrees F.

with how often vaccines should be given. Again, this seems to be different for each vaccine component. There seems to be general consensus that a puppy (or a dog with an unknown vaccination history) should get a series of vaccinations to initially stimulate his immunity and then a booster at one year of age, but, after that, even the veterinary associations and colleges have trouble reaching agreement. Rabies vaccination schedules are not debated, because vaccine schedules for this contagious and devastating disease are determined by government agencies. Regarding the rest, some recommend that we continue to give the vaccines annually because this method has worked well as a disease preventative for decades and delivers predictable protection. Others recommend that some of the vaccines only need to be given every second or third year, as this can be done without affecting levels of protection. This is probably true for some vaccine components (such as hepatitis), but there have been no large studies to demonstrate what the optimal interval should be and whether the same principles hold true for all breeds.

It may be best to just measure titers, which are protective blood levels of various vaccine components, on an annual basis, but that too is not without controversy. Scientists have not precisely determined the minimum titer of specific vaccine components that will be guaranteed to provide a pet with protection. Pets with very high titers will clearly be protected and those with very low titers will need repeat vaccinations, but there is also a large "gray zone" of pets that probably have intermediate protection and may or may not need repeat vaccination, depending on their risk of coming into contact with the disease.

These questions leave primary-care veterinarians in a very uncomfortable position, one that is not easy to resolve. Do they recommend annual vaccination in a manner that has demonstrated successful protection for decades, do they recommend skipping vaccines some years and hope that the protection lasts or do they measure blood tests (titers) and hope that the results are convincing enough to clearly indicate whether repeat vaccination is warranted?

These aren't the only vaccination questions impacting pets, owners and veterinarians. Other controversies focus on whether vaccines should be dosed according to body weight (currently they are administered in uniform doses, regardless of the animal's size), whether there are breed-specific issues important in determining vaccination programs (for instance, we know that some breeds have a harder time mounting an appropriate immune response to

BEER SUDS TO FOAMING DOGS: PASTEUR TO THE RESCUE

Rabies, as old as any plague, dates back to Babylonian days, the 23rd century BC. The term may derive from the Sanskrit word "rabhas," which translates "to do violence." In the 16th century, Girolama Fracastoro was the first scientist to describe the disease, which he did some 350 years prior to Louis Pasteur, the scientist well known in is his day for "pasteurizing" milk and beer.

In the 1870s, Pasteur emerged as a much-needed savior from terror in an irrational world. Ironically, his first effort in dealing with human disease was a vaccine for anthrax, which, like rabies, affects humans and animals alike. Rabies scourged Europe with a vengeance, and victims of the "violent virus" were either killed or committed suicide. Pasteur developed a vaccine for rabies by injecting brain material from a rabid dog into the bloodstream of a healthy dog. Once he developed a way of adjusting the virulence of the inoculation, he could build up the animal's resistance to the disease through a series of stronger inoculations. Since the virus developed slowly in an affected dog, the dog was able to develop immunity to the rabies before the incubation period had ended. After much experimentation, Pasteur was able to treat humans and, in 1885, his remarkable vaccination saved the first of millions of human beings.

parvovirus vaccine and might benefit from a different dose or injection interval) and which type of vaccine—live-virus or inactivated—offers more advantages with fewer disadvantages. Clearly, there are many more questions than there are answers. The important thing, as a pet owner, is to be aware of the issues and be able to work with your veterinarian to make decisions that are right for your pet. Be an informed consumer and you will appreciate the deliberation required in tailoring a vaccination program to best meet the needs of your pet. Expect also that this is an ongoing, ever-changing topic of debate; thus, the decisions you make this year won't necessarily be the same as the ones you make next year.

COMMON VACCINATIONS

Now that you are more confused than ever about vaccination, it is a good time to discuss some of the diseases that create the need for vaccination in the first place. Following are the major canine infectious diseases and a simple explanation of each.

Rabies is a devastating viral disease that can be fatal in dogs and people. In fact, vaccination of dogs and cats is an important public health measure to create a resistant animal buffer population to protect people from contracting the disease. Vaccination schedules are determined on a government level and are not optional for pet owners;

rabies vaccination is required by law in all 50 states.

Parvovirus is a severe, potentially life-threatening disease that is easily transmitted between dogs. There are four strains of the virus, but it is believed that there is significant "cross-protection" between strains that may be included in individual vaccines.

Distemper is another potentially severe and life-threatening disease with a relatively high risk of exposure, especially in certain regions. In very high-risk distemper environments, young pups may be vaccinated with human measles vaccine, a related virus that offers cross-

protection when administered at 4-10 weeks of age.

Hepatitis is caused by canine adenovirus type 1 (CAV-1), but since vaccination with the causative virus has a higher rate of adverse effects, cross-protection is derived from the use of adenovirus type 2 (CAV-2), a cause of respiratory disease and one of the potential causes of canine cough. Vaccination with CAV-2 provides long-term immunity against hepatitis but relatively less protection against respiratory infection.

Tracheobronchitis, commonly known as canine cough, is actually a fairly complicated result of viral and bacterial offenders; therefore,

SAMPLE VACCINATION SCHEDULE

6-8 weeks of age	Parvovirus, Distemper, Adenovirus-2 (Hepatitis)
9-11 weeks of age	Parvovirus, Distemper, Adenovirus-2 (Hepatitis)
12-14 weeks of age	Parvovirus, Distemper, Adenovirus-2 (Hepatitis)
16-20 weeks of age	Rabies
1 year of age	Parvovirus, Distemper, Adenovirus-2 (Hepatitis), Rabies

Revaccination is performed every one to three years, depending on the product, the method of administration and the patient's risk. Initial adult inoculation (for dogs at least 16 weeks of age in which a puppy series was not done or could not be confirmed) is two vaccinations, done three to four weeks apart, with revaccination according to the same criteria mentioned. Other vaccines are given as decided between owner and veterinarian.

even with vaccination, protection is incomplete. Wherever dogs congregate, canine cough will likely be spread among them. Intranasal vaccination with *Bordetella* and parainfluenza is the best safeguard, but the duration of immunity does not appear to be very long, typically a year at most. These are non-core vaccines, but vaccination is sometimes mandated by boarding kennels, obedience classes, dog shows and other places where dogs congregate to try to minimize spread of infection.

Leptospirosis is a potentially fatal disease that is more common in some geographic regions. It is capable of being spread to humans. The disease varies with the individual "serovar," or strain, of *Leptospira* involved; since there does not appear to be much cross-protection between serovars, protection is only as good as the likelihood that the serovar in the vaccine is the same as the one in the pet's local environment. Problems with *Leptospira* vaccines are that protection does not last very long, side effects are not uncommon and a large percentage of dogs (perhaps 30%) may not respond to vaccination.

Borrelia burgdorferi is the cause of **Lyme disease**, the risk of which varies with the geographic area in which the pet lives and travels. Lyme disease is spread by deer ticks in the eastern US and western black-legged ticks in the western

SIMULATED MEDICAL CONDITION FOR EDUCATIONAL PURPOSES ONLY.

part of the country, and the risk of exposure is high in some regions. Lameness, fever and inappetence are most commonly seen in affected dogs. The extent of protection from the vaccine has not been conclusively demonstrated.

Coronavirus has a high risk of exposure, especially in areas where dogs congregate, but it typically causes only mild to moderate digestive upset (diarrhea, vomiting, etc.). Vaccines are available, but the duration of protection is believed to be relatively short and the effectiveness of the vaccine in preventing infection is considered low.

There are many other vaccinations available, including those for *Giardia* and canine adenovirus-1. While there may be some specific indications for their use, and local risk factors to be considered, they are not widely recommended for most dogs.

An acral lick granuloma develops when the Bloodhound attacks a particular spot incessantly until it is raw and bleeding. Usually on his leg or paw, the syndrome can occur in a variety of locations.

NEUTERING/SPAYING

Sterilization procedures (neutering for males/spaying for females) are meant to accomplish several purposes. While the underlying premise is to address the risk of pet overpopulation, there are also some medical and behavioral benefits to the surgeries as well. For females, spaying prior to the first estrus (heat cycle) leads to a marked reduction in the risk of mammary cancer. There are also no manifestations of "heat" to attract male dogs nor bleeding in the house. For males, neutering prevents testicular cancer and reduces the risk of prostate problems. There may be some limited reduction in aggressive behaviors toward other dogs, and (as sex appropriate) some diminishing of urine marking, roaming and mounting.

While neutering and spaying do indeed prevent animals from contributing to pet overpopulation, even no-cost and low-cost neutering options have not eliminated the problem. Perhaps one of the main reasons for this is that individuals who intentionally breed their dogs and those who allow their animals to run at large are the main causes of unwanted offspring. Also, animals in shelters are often there because they were abandoned or relinquished, not because they came from unplanned matings. Neutering/spaying is important, but it should be considered in the context of the real causes of animals' ending up in shelters and eventually being euthanized.

One of the important considerations regarding sterilization is that it is a surgical procedure. This sometimes gets lost in discussions of low-cost procedures and commoditization of the process. In females, spaying is specifically referred to as an ovariohysterectomy. In this procedure, a midline incision is made in the abdomen and the entire uterus and both ovaries are surgically removed. While this is a major invasive surgical procedure, it usually has few complications, because it is typically performed on healthy young animals. However, it is a major surgery, as any woman who has had a hysterectomy will attest.

In males, neutering has traditionally referred to castration, which involves the surgical removal of both testicles. While still a significant piece of surgery, there is not the abdominal exposure that is required in the female surgery. In addition, there is now a chemical sterilization option, in which a solution is injected into each testicle, leading to atrophy of the sperm-producing cells. This can typically be done under sedation rather than full anesthesia. This is a relatively new approach, and there are no long-term clinical studies yet available.

Neutering/spaying is typically done around six months of age at most veterinary hospitals, although techniques have been pioneered to perform the procedures in animals as young as eight weeks of age. In general, the surgeries on the very young animals are done for the specific reason of sterilizing them before they go to their new homes. This is done in some shelter hospitals for assurance that the animals will definitely not produce any pups. Otherwise, these organizations need to rely on owners to comply with their wishes to have the animals "altered" at a later date, something that does not always happen.

There are some exciting immunocontraceptive "vaccines" currently under development, and there may be a time when contraception in pets will not require surgical procedures. We anxiously await these developments.

Puppies and adults alike can develop allergies related to their environment. Carefully consider the various plants and bushes to which your Bloodhound has access.

S. E. M. by Dr. Dennis Kunkel, University of Hawaii

A scanning electron micrograph of a dog flea, *Ctenocephalides canis*, on dog hair.

EXTERNAL PARASITES

FLEAS

Fleas have been around for millions of years and, while we have better tools now for controlling them than at any time in the past, there still is little chance that they will end up on an endangered species list. Actually, they are very well adapted to living on our pets, and they continue to adapt as we make advances.

The female flea can consume 15 times her weight in blood during active reproduction and can lay as many as 40 eggs a day. These eggs are very resistant to the effects of insecticides. They hatch into larvae, which then mature and spin cocoons. The immature fleas reside in this pupal stage until the time is right for feeding. This pupal stage is also very resistant to the effects of insecticides, and pupae can last in the environment without feeding for many months. Newly emergent fleas are attracted to animals by the warmth of the animals' bodies, movement and exhaled carbon dioxide. However, when they first emerge from their cocoons, they orient towards light; thus, when an animal passes between a flea and the light source, casting a shadow, the flea pounces and starts to feed. If the animal turns out to be a dog or cat, the reproductive cycle continues. If the flea lands on another type of animal, including a person, the flea will bite but will then look for a more appropriate host. An emerging adult flea can survive without feeding for up to 12 months but, once it tastes blood, it can only survive off its host for three to four days.

It was once thought that fleas spend most of their lives in the environment, but we now know that fleas won't willingly jump off a dog unless leaping to another dog or when physically removed by brushing, bathing or other manipulation. Flea eggs, on the other hand, are shiny and smooth, and they roll off the animal and into the environment. The eggs, larvae and pupae then exist in the environment, but once the adult finds a susceptible animal, it's home sweet home until the flea is convinced to seek refuge elsewhere.

Since adult fleas live on the animal and immature forms survive in the environment, a successful treatment plan must address all stages of the flea life cycle. There are now several safe and effective flea-control products that can be applied on a monthly

FLEA PREVENTION FOR YOUR DOG
- Discuss with your veterinarian the safest product to protect your dog, likely in the form of a monthly tablet or a liquid preparation placed on the back of the dog's neck.
- For dogs suffering from flea-bite dermatitis, a shampoo or topical insecticide treatment is required.
- Your lawn and property should be sprayed with an insecticide designed to kill fleas and ticks that lurk outdoors.
- Using a flea comb, check the dog's coat regularly for any signs of parasites.
- Practice good housekeeping: vacuum floors, carpets and furniture regularly, especially in the areas that the dog frequents, and wash the dog's bedding weekly.
- Follow up house-cleaning with carpet shampoos and sprays to rid the house of fleas at all stages of development. Insect growth regulators are the safest option.

basis. These include fipronil, imidacloprid, selamectin and permethrin (found in several formulations). Most of these products have significant flea-killing rates within 24 hours. However, none of them will control the immature forms in the environment. To accomplish this, there are a variety of insect growth regulators that can be sprayed into

THE FLEA'S LIFE CYCLE

What came first, the flea or the egg? This age-old mystery is more difficult to comprehend than the

actual cycle of the flea. Fleas usually live only about four months. A female can lay 2,000 eggs in her lifetime.

Egg

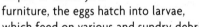

After ten days of rolling around your carpet or under your furniture, the eggs hatch into larvae,

Larva

which feed on various and sundry debris. In days or

months, depending on the climate, the larvae spin a cocoon and develop into the pupal or nymph stage, which quickly develop into fleas.

Pupa

These immature fleas must locate a host within 10 to 14 days or they will die. Only about 1% of the flea population exist as adult fleas, while the other 99% exist as eggs, larvae or pupae.

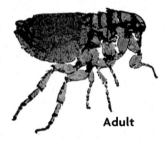

Adult

KILL FLEAS THE NATURAL WAY

If you choose not to go the route of conventional medication, there are some natural ways to ward off fleas:

- Dust your dog with a natural flea powder, comprised of such herbal goodies as rosemary, wormwood, pennyroyal, citronella, rue, tobacco powder and eucalyptus.
- Apply diatomaceous earth, the fossilized remains of single-cell algae, to your carpets, furniture and pet's bedding. Even though it's not good for dogs, it's even worse for fleas, which will dry up swiftly and die.
- Brush your dog frequently, give him adequate exercise and let him fast occasionally. All of these activities strengthen the dog's system and make him more resistant to disease and parasites.
- Bathe your dog with a capful of pennyroyal or eucalyptus oil.
- Feed a natural diet, free of additives and preservatives. Add some fresh garlic and brewer's yeast to the dog's morning portion, as these have flea-repelling properties.

the environment (e.g., pyriprox-yfen, methoprene, fenoxycarb) as well as insect development inhibitors such as lufenuron that can be administered. These compounds have no effect on adult fleas, but they stop immature forms from developing into adults. In years gone by, we relied heavily on toxic insecti-cides (such as organophosphates, organochlorines and carbamates) to manage the flea problem, but today's options are not only much safer to use on our pets but also safer for the environment.

TICKS

Ticks are members of the spider group (arachnids) and are blood-sucking parasites capable of transmitting a variety of diseases, including Lyme disease, ehrlichiosis, babesiosis and Rocky Mountain spotted fever. It's easy to see ticks on your own skin, but it is more of a challenge when your furry companion is affected. Whenever you happen to be planning a stroll in a tick-infested area (especially forests, grassy or wooded areas or parks) be prepared to do a thorough inspection of your dog afterward to search for ticks. Ticks can be tricky, so make sure you spend time looking in the ears, between the toes and everywhere else where a tick might hide. Ticks need to be attached for 24–72 hours before they transmit most of the diseases that they carry, so you do have a window of opportunity for some preventative intervention.

A TICKING BOMB

There is nothing good about a tick harpooning his nose into your dog's skin. Among the diseases caused by ticks are Rocky Mountain spotted fever, canine ehrlichiosis, canine babesiosis, canine hepatozoonosis and Lyme disease. If a dog is allergic to the saliva of a female wood tick, he can develop tick paralysis.

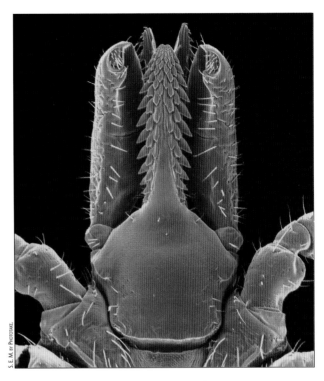

S. E. M. BY PHOTOTAKE.

Female ticks live to eat and breed. They can lay between 4,000 and 5,000 eggs and they die soon after. Males, on the other hand, live only to mate with other females and continue the process as long as they are able. Most ticks live on multiple hosts before parasitizing dogs. The immature forms typically reside on grass and shrubs, waiting for susceptible animals to walk by. The larvae and nymph stages typically feed on wildlife.

If only a few ticks are present on a dog, they can be plucked out, but it is important to remove the entire head and mouthparts,

A scanning electron micrograph of the head of a female deer tick, *Ixodes dammini,* a parasitic tick that carries Lyme disease.

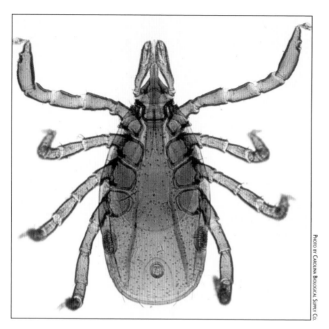

PHOTO BY CAROLINA BIOLOGICAL SUPPLY CO.

Deer tick,
Ixodes dammini.

which may be deeply embedded in the skin. This is best accomplished with forceps designed especially for this purpose; fingers can be used, but should be protected with rubber gloves, plastic wrap or at least a paper towel. The tick should be grasped as closely as possible to the animal's skin and should be pulled upward with steady, even pressure. Do not squeeze, crush or puncture the body of the tick or you risk exposure to any disease carried by that tick. Once the ticks have been removed, the sites of attachment should be disinfected. Your hands should then be washed with soap and water to further minimize risk of contagion. The tick should be disposed of in a container of alcohol or flushed down the toilet.

Some of the newer flea products, specifically those with fipronil, selamectin and permethrin, have effect against some, but not all, species of tick. Flea collars containing appropriate insecticides (e.g., propoxur, chlorfenvinphos) can aid in tick control. In most areas, such collars should be placed on animals in March, at the beginning of the tick season, and changed regularly. Leaving the collar on when the insecticide level is waning invites the development of resistance. Amitraz collars are also good for tick control, and the active ingredient does not interfere with other flea-control products. The ingredient helps prevent the attachment of ticks to the skin and will cause those ticks already on the skin to detach themselves.

TICK CONTROL

Removal of underbrush and leaf litter and the thinning of trees in areas where tick control is desired are recommended. These actions remove the cover and food sources for small animals that serve as hosts for ticks. With continued mowing of grasses in these areas, the probability of ticks' surviving is further reduced. A variety of insecticide ingredients (e.g., resmethrin, carbaryl, permethrin, chlorpyrifos, dioxathion and allethrin) are registered for tick control around the home.

MITES

Mites are tiny arachnid parasites that parasitize the skin of dogs. Skin diseases caused by mites are referred to as "mange," and there are many different forms seen in dogs. These forms are very different from one another, each one warranting an individual description.

Sarcoptic mange, or scabies, is one of the itchiest conditions that affects dogs. The microscopic *Sarcoptes* mites burrow into the superficial layers of the skin and can drive dogs crazy with itchiness. They are also communicable to people, although they can't complete their reproductive cycle on people. Not only are the mites tiny but also are often difficult to find when trying to make a diagnosis. Skin scrapings from multiple areas are examined microscopically but, even then, sometimes the mites cannot be found.

Fortunately, scabies is relatively easy to treat, and there are a variety of products that will successfully kill the mites. Since the mites can't live in the environment for very long without feeding, a complete cure is usually possible within four to eight weeks.

Cheyletiellosis is caused by a relatively large mite, which sometimes can be seen even without a microscope. Often referred to as "walking dandruff," this also causes itching, but not usually as profound as with scabies.

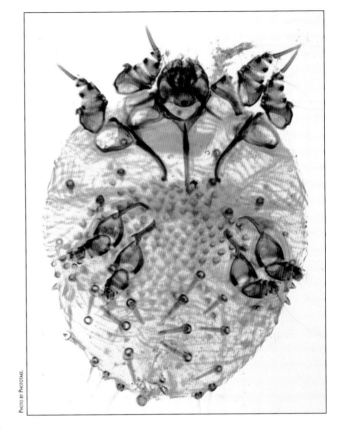

PHOTO BY PHOTOTAKE.

Sarcoptes scabiei, commonly known as the "itch mite."

While *Cheyletiella* mites can survive somewhat longer in the environment than scabies mites, they too are relatively easy to treat, being responsive not only to the medications used to treat scabies but also often to flea-control products.

Otodectes cynotis is the cause of ear mites and is one of the more common causes of mange, especially in young dogs in shelters or pet stores. That's because the mites are typically present in large

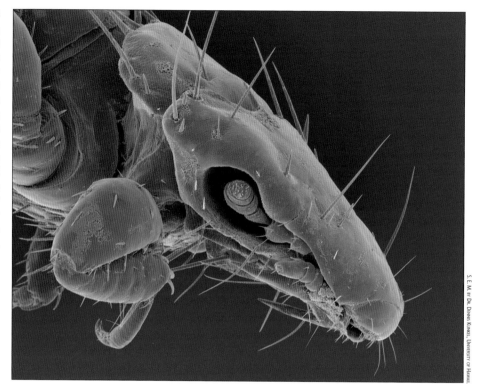

Micrograph of a dog louse, *Heterodoxus spiniger*. Female lice attach their eggs to the hairs of the dog. As the eggs hatch, the larval lice bite and feed on the blood. Lice can also feed on dead skin and hair. This feeding activity can cause hair loss and skin problems.

S. E. M. by Dr. Dennis Kunkel, University of Hawaii

numbers and are quickly spread to nearby animals. The mites rarely do much harm, but can be difficult to eradicate if the treatment regimen is not comprehensive. While many try to treat the condition with ear drops only, this is the most common cause of treatment failure. Ear drops cause the mites to simply move out of the ears and as far away as possible (usually to the base of the tail) until the insecticide levels in the ears drop to an acceptable level—then it's back to business as usual! The successful treatment of ear mites requires treating all animals in the household with a systemic insecti-cide, such as selamectin, or a combination of miticidal ear drops combined with whole-body flea-control preparations.

Demodicosis, sometimes referred to as red mange, can be one of the most difficult forms of mange to treat. Part of the problem has to do with the fact that the mites live in the hair follicles and are relatively well shielded from topical and systemic products. The main issue, however, is that demodectic mange typically only results when there is some underlying process interfering with the dog's immune system.

Since *Demodex* mites are

normal residents of the skin of mammals, including humans, there is usually only a mite population explosion when the immune system fails to keep the number of mites in check. In young animals, the immune deficit may be transient or it may reflect an actual inherited immune problem. In older animals, demodicosis is usually seen only when there is another disease hampering the immune system, such as diabetes, cancer, thyroid problems or the use of immune-suppressing drugs. Accordingly, treatment involves not only trying to kill the mange mites but also discerning what is interfering with immune function and correcting it if possible.

Chiggers represent several different species of mite that don't parasitize dogs specifically, but do latch on to passersby and can cause irritation. The problem is most prevalent in wooded areas in the late summer and fall. Treatment is not difficult, as the mites do not complete their life cycle on dogs and are susceptible to a variety of insecticides.

ILLUSTRATION BY PHOTOTAKE

MOSQUITOES

Mosquitoes have long been known to transmit a variety of diseases to people, as well as just being biting pests during warm weather. They also pose a real risk to pets. Not only do they carry deadly heartworms but recently there also has been much concern over their involvement with West Nile virus. While we can avoid heartworm with the use of preventive medications, there are no such preventives for West Nile virus. The only method of prevention in endemic areas is active mosquito control. Fortunately, most dogs that have been exposed to the virus only developed flu-like symptoms and, to date, there have not been the large number of reported deaths in canines as seen in some other species.

Illustration of
*Demodex
folliculoram V.*

MOSQUITO REPELLENT

Low concentrations of DEET (less than 10%), found in many human mosquito repellents, have been safely used in dogs but, in these concentrations, probably only give about two hours of protection. DEET may be safe in these small concentrations, but since it is not licensed for use on dogs, there is no research proving its safety for dogs. Products containing permethrin give the longest-lasting protection, perhaps two to four weeks. As DEET is not licensed for use on dogs, and both DEET and permethrin can be quite toxic to cats, appropriate care should be exercised. Other products, such as those containing oil of citronella, also have some mosquito-repellent activity, but typically have relatively short duration of action.

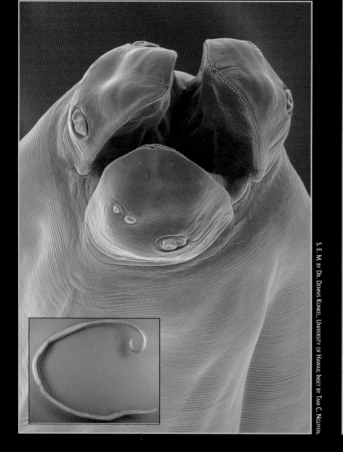

S. E. M. by Dr. Dennis Kunkel, University of Hawaii. Inset by Tam C. Nguyen.

ASCARID DANGERS
The most commonly encountered worm in dogs is the roundworm, known as the ascarid. *Toxascaris leonine* and *Toxocara canis* are the two species that infect dogs. Subsisting in the dog's stomach and intestines, adult roundworms can grow to 7 inches in length and adult females can lay in excess of 200,000 eggs in a single day.

In humans, visceral larva migrans affects people who have ingested eggs of *Toxocara canis*, which frequently contaminate children's sandboxes, beaches and park grounds. The roundworms reside in the human's stomach and intestines, as they would in a dog's, but do not mature. Instead, they find their way to the liver, lungs and skin, or even to the heart or kidneys in severe cases. Deworming puppies is critical in preventing the infection in humans, and young children should never handle nursing pups who have not been dewormed.

Roundworm, *Toxocara canis*, showing the mouth with three lips. Inset: Photomicrograph of a roundworm, *Ascaris lumbricoides*.

INTERNAL PARASITES

ROUNDWORMS

Roundworms are intestinal parasites that rarely cause severe disease in dogs. Nonetheless, they are of major public health significance because they can be transferred to people. Sadly, it is children who are most commonly affected with the parasite, probably from inadvertently ingesting roundworm-contaminated soil. In fact, many yards and children's sandboxes contain appreciable numbers of roundworm eggs. So while roundworms don't bite dogs or latch on to their intestines to suck blood, they do cause some nasty medical conditions in children and are best eradicated from our furry friends. Because pups can start passing roundworm eggs by three weeks of age, most parasite-control programs begin at two weeks of age and are repeated every two weeks until pups are eight weeks old. It is important to

HOOKED ON ANCYLOSTOMA

Adult dogs can become infected by the bloodsucking nematodes we commonly call hookworms via ingesting larvae from the ground or via the larvae penetrating the dog's skin. It is not uncommon for infected dogs to show no symptoms of hookworm infestation. Sometimes, symptoms occur within ten days of exposure. These symptoms can include bloody diarrhea, anemia, loss of weight and general weakness. Dogs pass the hookworm eggs in their stools, which serves as the vet's method of identifying the infestation. The hookworm larvae can encyst themselves in the dog's tissues and be released when the dog is experiencing stress.

Caused by *Ancylostoma braziliense*, whose common host is the dog, cutaneous larva migrans affects humans, causing itching and lumps and streaks beneath the surface of the skin.

S. E. M. by Dr. Dennis Kunkel, University of Hawaii.

realize that bitches can pass roundworms to their pups even if they test negative prior to whelping. Accordingly, bitches are best treated at the same time as the pups.

HOOKWORMS

Unlike roundworms, hookworms do latch on to a dog's intestinal tract and can cause significant loss of blood and protein. Similar to roundworms, hookworms can be transmitted to humans, where they cause a condition known as cutaneous larva migrans. Dogs can become infected either by consuming the infective larvae or by the larvae's penetrating the skin directly. People most often get infected when they are lying on the ground (such as on a beach) and the larvae penetrate the skin. Yes, the larvae can penetrate through a beach blanket. Hookworms are typically susceptible to the same medications used to treat roundworms.

Hookworm, *Ancylostoma caninum*, a small parasitic worm about 1 mm inn length at full size. Inset: Posterior end of a male hookworm.

WHIPWORMS

Whipworms latch on to the lower aspects of the dog's colon and can cause cramping and diarrhea. Eggs do not start to appear in the dog's feces until about three months after the dog was infected. This worm has a peculiar life cycle, which makes it more difficult to control than roundworms or hookworms. The good thing is that whipworms rarely are transferred to people.

Some of the medications used to treat roundworms and hookworms are also effective against whipworms, but, in general, a separate treatment protocol is needed. Since most of the medications are effective against the adults but not the eggs or larvae, treatment is typically repeated in three weeks,

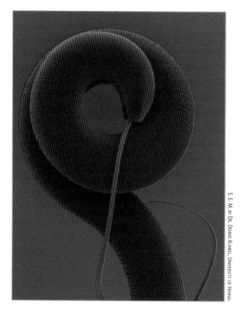

Adult whipworm, *Trichuris sp.*, an intestinal parasite.

S. E. M. BY DR. DENNIS KUNKEL, UNIVERSITY OF HAWAII.

WORM-CONTROL GUIDELINES

- Practice sanitary habits with your dog and home.
- Clean up after your dog and don't let him sniff or eat other dogs' droppings.
- Control insects and fleas in the dog's environment. Fleas, lice, cockroaches, beetles, mice and rats can act as hosts for various worms.
- Prevent dogs from eating uncooked meat, raw poultry and dead animals.
- Keep dogs and children from playing in sand and soil.
- Kennel dogs on cement or gravel; avoid dirt runs.
- Administer heartworm preventatives regularly.
- Have your vet examine your dog's stools at your annual visits.
- Select a boarding kennel carefully, so as to avoid contamination from other dogs or an unsanitary environment.
- Prevent dogs from roaming. Obey local leash laws.

and then often in three months as well. Unfortunately, since dogs don't develop resistance to whipworms, it is difficult to prevent them from getting reinfected if they visit soil contaminated with whipworm eggs.

TAPEWORMS

There are many different species of tapeworm that affect dogs, but *Dipylidium caninum* is probably the most common and is spread by fleas. Flea larvae feed on organic debris and tapeworm eggs in the environment and, when a dog chews at himself and manages to ingest fleas, he might get a dose of tapeworm at the same time. The tapeworm then develops further in the intestine of the dog.

The tapeworm itself, which latches on to the intestinal wall, is composed of numerous segments. When the segments break off into the intestine (as proglottids), they may accumulate around the rectum, like grains of rice. While this tapeworm is disgusting in its behavior, it is not directly communicable to humans (although humans can also get infected by swallowing fleas).

A much more dangerous tapeworm is *Echinococcus multilocularis*, which is typically found in foxes, coyotes and wolves. The eggs are passed in the feces and infect rodents, and, when dogs eat the rodents, the dogs can be infected by thousands of adult tapeworms. While the parasites don't cause many problems in dogs, this is considered the most lethal worm infection that people can get. Take appropriate precautions if you live in an area in which these tapeworms are found. Do not use mulch that may contain feces of dogs, cats or wildlife, and

discourage your pets from hunting wildlife. Treat these tapeworm infections aggressively in pets, because if humans get infected, approximately half die.

HEARTWORMS

Heartworm disease is caused by the parasite *Dirofilaria immitis* and is seen in dogs around the world. The parasite itself, an actual worm, is spread between dogs by the bite of an infected mosquito. The mosquito injects infective larvae into the dog's skin with its bite, and these larvae develop under the skin for a period of time before making their way to the heart. There they develop into adults, which grow and create blockage of the heart, lungs and major blood vessels there. They also start

Dog tapeworm proglottid (body segment).

Dog tapeworm, *Taenia pisiformis*.

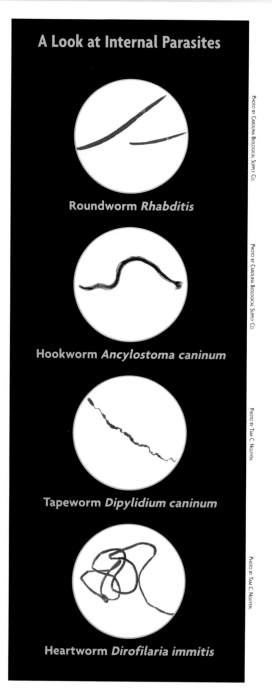

A Look at Internal Parasites

Roundworm *Rhabditis*

Hookworm *Ancylostoma caninum*

Tapeworm *Dipylidium caninum*

Heartworm *Dirofilaria immitis*

PHOTO BY CAROLINA BIOLOGICAL SUPPLY CO.

PHOTO BY CAROLINA BIOLOGICAL SUPPLY CO.

PHOTO BY TAM C. NGUYEN.

PHOTO BY TAM C. NGUYEN.

producing offspring (microfilariae) and these microfilariae circulate in the bloodstream, waiting to hitch a ride when the next mosquito bites. Once in the mosquito, the microfilariae develop into infective larvae and the entire process is repeated.

When dogs get infected with heartworm, over time they tend to develop symptoms associated with heart disease, such as coughing, exercise intolerance and potentially many other manifestations. Diagnosis is confirmed by either seeing the microfilariae themselves in blood samples or using immunologic tests (antigen testing) to identify the presence of adult heartworms. Since antigen tests measure the presence of adult heartworms, and microfilarial tests measure offspring produced by adults, neither are positive until six to seven months after the initial infection. However, the beginning of damage can occur by fifth-stage larvae as early as three months after infection. Thus it is possible for dogs to be harboring problem-causing larvae for up to three months before either type of test would identify an infection.

The good news is that there are great protocols available for preventing heartworm in dogs. Testing is critical in the process, and it is important to understand the benefits as well as the limitations of such testing. All dogs six months of age or older that have not been on continuous heartworm-preventive

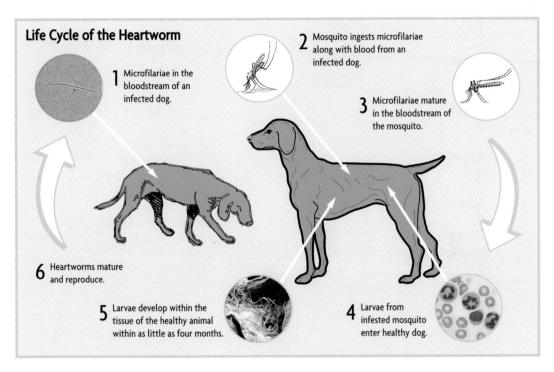

Life Cycle of the Heartworm

1 Microfilariae in the bloodstream of an infected dog.

2 Mosquito ingests microfilariae along with blood from an infected dog.

3 Microfilariae mature in the bloodstream of the mosquito.

4 Larvae from infested mosquito enter healthy dog.

5 Larvae develop within the tissue of the healthy animal within as little as four months.

6 Heartworms mature and reproduce.

medication should be screened with microfilarial or antigen tests. For dogs receiving preventive medication, periodic antigen testing helps assess the effectiveness of the preventives. The American Heartworm Society guidelines suggest that annual retesting may not be necessary when owners have absolutely provided continuous heartworm prevention. Retesting on a two- to three-year interval may be sufficient in these cases. However, your vet will likely have specific guidelines under which heartworm preventives will be prescribed, and many prefer to err on the side of safety and retest annually.

It is indeed fortunate that heartworm is relatively easy to prevent, because treatments can be as life-threatening as the disease itself. Treatment requires a two-step process that kills the adult heartworms first and then the microfilariae. Prevention is obviously preferable; this involves a once-monthly oral or topical treatment. The most common oral preventives include ivermectin (not suitable for some breeds), moxidectin and milbemycin oxime; the once-a-month topical drug selamectin provides heartworm protection in addition to flea, tick and other parasite controls.

BLOODHOUND

When we bring home a puppy, full of the energy and exuberance that accompanies youth, we hope for a long, happy and fulfilling relationship with the new family member. Even when we adopt an older dog, we look forward to the years of companionship ahead with a new canine friend. However, aging is inevitable for all creatures, and there will come a time when our dog reaches his senior years and will need special considerations and attention to his care.

WHEN IS MY DOG A "SENIOR?"
Dogs generally are considered "seniors" at seven years of age, but that is not always accurate. A dog's senior status is better determined based on the average life expectancy for his breed, which is based on the size of the breed. Average life expectancies are considered as follows: small breeds, 12 years or more; medium breeds, 10 years or more; large breeds, 9 years or more and giant breeds, 7 years or more. A dog is considered a senior when he has reached 75% of the average lifespan for his breed. Your Bloodhound has an average lifespan of ten years, though some Bloodhounds only lives six or seven years.

Thus, the old "seven dog years to one human year" theory is not exact. In puppyhood, a dog's year is actually comparable to more than seven human years, considering the puppy's rapid growth during his first year. Then, in adulthood, the ratio decreases. Regardless, a more viable rule of thumb is that the larger the dog, the shorter his expected lifespan. Of course, this can vary among individual dogs, with many living longer than expected, which we hope is the case!

WHAT ARE THE SIGNS OF AGING?
By the time your dog has reached his senior years, you will know him very well and, thus, the physical and behavioral changes that accompany aging should be noticeable to you. Humans and dogs share the most obvious physical sign of aging: gray hair! Graying often occurs first on the muzzle and face, around the eyes. Other telltale signs are the dog's overall decrease in activity. Your older dog might be more content

to nap and rest, and he may not show the same old enthusiasm when it's time to play in the yard or go for a walk. Other physical signs include significant weight loss or gain; more labored movement; skin and coat problems, possibly hair loss; sight and/or hearing problems; changes in toileting habits, perhaps seeming "unhousebroken" at times; tooth decay, bad breath or other mouth problems.

There are behavioral changes that go along with aging, too. There are numerous causes for behavioral changes. Sometimes a dog's apparent confusion results from a physical change like diminished sight or hearing. If his confusion causes him to be afraid, he may act aggressively or defensively. He may sleep more frequently because his daily walks, though shorter now, tire him out. He may begin to experience separation anxiety or, conversely, become less interested in petting and attention.

There also are clinical conditions that cause behavioral changes in older dog. One such condition is known as canine cognitive dysfunction (familiarly known as "old-dog" syndrome). It can be frustrating for an owner

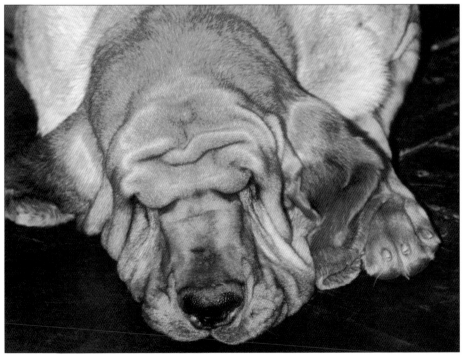

Senior Bloodhounds will sleep more frequently and for longer periods. No two dogs age at the exact same rate, so each Bloodhound will need to be accessed by a vet to determine what modifications in his diet and care regimen are advisable.

whose dog is affected with cognitive dysfunction, as it can result in behavioral changes of all types, most seemingly unexplainable. Common changes include the dog's forgetting aspects of the daily routine, such as times to eat, go out for walks, relieve himself and the like. Along the same lines, you may take your dog out at the regular time for a potty trip and he may have no idea why he is there. Sometimes a placid dog will begin to show aggressive or possessive tendencies or, conversely, a hyperactive dog will start to "mellow out."

Disease also can be the cause of behavioral changes in senior dogs. Hormonal problems (Cushing's disease is common in older dogs), diabetes and thyroid disease can cause increased appetite, which can lead to aggression related to food guarding. It's better to be proactive with your senior dog, making more frequent trips to the vet if necessary and having bloodwork done to test for the diseases that can commonly befall older dogs.

This is not to say that, as dogs age, they all fall apart physically and become nasty in personality. The aforementioned changes are discussed to alert owners to the things that *may* happen as their dogs get older. Many hardy dogs remain active and alert well into old age. However, it can be frustrating and heartbreaking for owners to see their beloved dogs change physically and temperamentally. Just know that it's the same dog under there and that he still loves you and appreciates your care, which he needs now more than ever.

HOW DO I CARE FOR MY AGING DOG?

Again, every dog is an individual in terms of aging. Your dog might reach the estimated "senior" age for his breed and show no signs of slowing down. However, even if he shows no outward signs of aging, he should begin a senior-care program once he reaches the determined age. He may not show it, but he's not a pup anymore! By providing him with extra attention to his veterinary care at this age, you will be practicing good preventive medicine, ensuring that the rest of your dog's life will be as long, active, happy and healthy as possible. If you do notice indications of aging, such as graying and/or changes in sleeping, eating or toileting habits, this is a sign to set up a senior-care visit with your vet right away to make sure that these changes are not related to any health problems.

To start, senior dogs should visit the vet twice yearly for exams, routine tests and overall evaluations. Many veterinarians have special screening programs

AH, MY ACHING BONES!

As your pet ages, and things that once were routine become difficult for him to handle, you may need to make some adjustments around the home to make things easier for your dog. Senior dogs affected by arthritis may have trouble moving about. If you notice this in your dog, you may have to limit him to one floor of the house so that he does not have to deal with stairs. If there are a few steps leading out into the yard, a ramp may help the dog. Likewise, he may need a ramp or a boost to get in and out of the car. Ensure that he has plenty of soft bedding on which to sleep and rest, as this will be comfortable for his aching joints. Also ensure that surfaces on which the dog walks are not slippery. Investigate new dietary supplements made for arthritic dogs. Studies have found that products containing glucosamine added once or twice daily to the senior dog's food can have beneficial effects on the dog's joints. Many of these products also contain natural anti-inflammatories such as chondroitin, MSM and cetyl myristoleate, as well as natural herbal remedies and nutmeg. Talk to your vet about these supplements.

dental exams. With these tests, it can be determined whether your dog has any health problems; the results also establish a baseline for your pet against which future test results can be compared.

In addition to these tests, your vet may suggest additional testing, including an EKG, tests for glaucoma and other problems of the eye, chest X-rays, screening for tumors, blood pressure test, test for thyroid function and screening for parasites and reassessment of his preventive program. Your vet also will ask you questions about your dog's diet and activity level, what you feed and the amounts that you feed. This information, along with his evaluation of the dog's overall condition, will enable him to suggest proper dietary changes, if needed.

This may seem like quite a work-up for your pet, but veterinarians advise that older dogs need more frequent attention so that any health problems can be detected as early as possible. Serious conditions like kidney disease, heart disease and cancer may not present outward symptoms, or the problem may go undetected if the symptoms are mistaken by owners as just part of the aging process.

There are some conditions more common in elderly dogs that are difficult to ignore. Cognitive dysfunction shares much in

especially for senior dogs that can include a thorough physical exam; blood test to determine complete blood count; serum biochemistry test, which screens for liver, kidney and blood problems as well as cancer; urinalysis; and

common with senility and Alzheimer's disease, and dogs are not immune. Dogs can become confused and/or disoriented, lose their house-training, have abnormal sleep/wake cycles and interact differently with their owners. Be heartened by the fact that, in some ways, there are more treatment options for dogs with cognitive dysfunction than for people with similar conditions. There is good evidence that continued stimulation in the form of games, play, training and exercise can help to maintain cognitive function. There are also medications (such as seligiline) and antioxidant-fortified senior diets that have been shown to be beneficial.

Cancer is also a condition more common in the elderly. Almost all of the cancers seen in people are also seen in pets. While we can't control the effects of second-hand smoke, lung cancer, which is a major killer in humans, is relatively rare in dogs. If pets are getting regular physical examinations, cancers are often detected early. There are a variety of cancer therapies available today and many pets continue to live happy lives with appropriate treatment.

Degenerative joint disease, often referred to as arthritis, is another common malady shared between elderly dogs and humans. A lifetime of wear and tear on joints and running around at play eventually takes its toll and results in stiffness and difficulty getting around. As dogs live longer and healthier lives, it is natural that they should eventually feel some of the effects of aging. Once again, if regular veterinary care has been available, your pet was not carrying extra pounds all those years and wearing those joints out before their time. If your pet was unfortunate enough to inherit hip dysplasia, osteochondrosis dissecans or any of the other developmental orthopedic diseases, battling the onset of degenerative joint disease was probably a longstanding goal. In any case, there are now many effective remedies for managing degenerative joint disease and a number of remarkable surgeries as well.

Hopefully, you've been regular with brushing your dog's teeth throughout his life. Healthy teeth directly affect overall good health. We already know that bacteria from gum infections can enter the dog's body through the damaged gums and travel to the organs. At a stage in life when his organs don't function as well as they used to, you don't want anything to put additional strain on them. Clean teeth also contribute to a healthy immune system. Offering the dental-type chews in addition to toothbrushing can help, as they

CDS: COGNITIVE DYSFUNCTION SYNDROME
"Old-Dog Syndrome"

There are many ways for you to evaluate old-dog syndrome. Veterinarians have defined CDS (cognitive dysfunction syndrome) as the gradual deterioration of cognitive abilities, indicated by changes in the dog's behavior. When a dog changes his routine response, and maladies have been eliminated as the cause of these behavioral changes, then CDS is the usual diagnosis.

More than half the dogs over eight years old suffer from some form of CDS. The older the dog, the more chance he has of suffering from CDS. In humans, doctors often dismiss the CDS behavioral changes as part of "winding down."

There are four major signs of CDS: frequent potty accidents inside the home, sleeping much more or much less than normal, acting confused and failing to respond to social stimuli.

SYMPTOMS OF CDS

FREQUENT POTTY ACCIDENTS
- *Urinates in the house.*
- *Defecates in the house.*
- *Doesn't signal that he wants to go out.*

SLEEP PATTERNS
- *Awakens more slowly.*
- *Sleeps more than normal during the day.*
- *Sleeps less during the night.*

CONFUSION
- *Goes outside and just stands there.*
- *Appears confused with a faraway look in his eyes.*
- *Hides more often.*
- *Doesn't recognize friends.*
- *Doesn't come when called.*
- *Walks around listlessly and without a destination.*

FAILURE TO RESPOND TO SOCIAL STIMULI
- *Comes to people less frequently, whether called or not.*
- *Doesn't tolerate petting for more than a short time.*
- *Doesn't come to the door when you return home.*

remove plaque and tartar as the dog chews.

Along with the same good care you've given him all of his life, pay a little extra attention to your dog in his senior years and keep up with twice-yearly trips to the vet. The sooner a problem is uncovered, the greater the chances of a full recovery.

SAYING GOODBYE
While you can help your dog live as long a life as possible, you can't help him live forever. A dog's lifespan is short when compared to that of a human, so it is inevitable that pet owners will experience loss. To many, losing a beloved dog is like losing a family member. Our dogs are part of our lives every day, are our true loyal friends and always seem to know when it's time to comfort us, to celebrate with us or to just provide the company of a caring friend. Even if we know that our dog is nearing his final days, we can never quite prepare for his being gone.

Many dogs live out long lives and simply die of old age. Others unfortunately are taken suddenly by illness or accident, and still others find their senior years compromised by disease and physical problems. In some of these cases, owners find themselves having to make difficult decisions.

Many cities have pet cemeteries conveniently located. Your vet can assist you in locating one.

BLOODHOUND

Is dog showing in your blood? Are you excited by the idea of gaiting your handsome Bloodhound around the ring to the thunderous applause of an enthusiastic audience? Are you certain that your beloved Bloodhound is flawless? You are not alone! Every loving owner thinks that his dog has no faults, or too few to mention. No matter how many times an owner reads over the breed standard, he cannot find any faults in his aristocratic companion dog. If this sounds like you, and if you are considering entering your Bloodhound in a dog show, here are some basic questions to ask yourself:

- Did you purchase a "show-quality" puppy from the breeder?
- Is your puppy at least six months of age?
- Does the puppy exhibit correct show type for his breed?
- Does your puppy have any disqualifying faults?
- Is your Bloodhound registered with the American Kennel Club?
- How much time do you have to devote to training, grooming, conditioning and exhibiting your dog?
- Do you understand the rules and regulations of a dog show?
- Do you have time to learn how to show your dog properly?
- Do you have the financial resources to invest in showing your dog?
- Will you show the dog yourself or hire a professional handler?
- Do you have a vehicle that can accommodate your weekend trips to the dog shows?

Success in the show ring requires more than a pretty face, a waggy tail and a pocketful of liver. Even though dog shows can be exciting and enjoyable, the sport of conformation makes great

BECOMING A CHAMPION
An official AKC champion of record requires that a dog accumulate 15 points under three different judges, including two "majors" under different judges. Points are awarded based on the number of dogs entered into competition, varying from breed to breed and place to place. A win of three, four or five points is considered a "major." The AKC annually assigns a schedule of points to adjust the variations that accompany a breed's popularity and the population of a given area.

FOR MORE INFORMATION....

For reliable, up-to-date information about registration, dog shows and other canine competitions, contact one of the national registries by mail or via the Internet.

American Kennel Club
5580 Centerview Dr., Raleigh, NC 27606-3390
www.akc.org

United Kennel Club
100 E. Kilgore Road, Kalamazoo, MI 49002
www.ukcdogs.com

Canadian Kennel Club
89 Skyway Ave., Suite 100, Etobicoke, Ontario
M9W 6R4 Canada
www.ckc.ca

The Kennel Club
1-5 Clarges St., Piccadilly, London W1Y 8AB,
UK
www.the-kennel-club.org.uk

purchased a puppy of the correct type and quality for showing, let's begin to examine the world of showing and what's required to get started. Although the entry fee into a dog show is nominal, there are lots of other hidden costs involved with "finishing" your Bloodhound, that is, making him a champion. Things like equipment, travel, training and conditioning all cost money. A more serious campaign will include fees for a professional handler, boarding, cross-country travel and advertising. Top-winning show dogs represent an investment of over $100,000 per year. Keep in mind that few dog shows offer cash prizes! For the 100,000 reasons listed above, many dog owners are opting to participate in United Kennel Club shows, where professional handlers are not permitted. These shows are more owner-oriented and, for many, more rewarding than AKC events.

demands on the exhibitors and the dogs. Winning exhibitors live for their dogs, devoting time and money to their dogs' presentation, conditioning and training. Very few novices, even those with good dogs, will find themselves in the winners' circle, though it does happen. Don't be disheartened, though. Every exhibitor began as a novice and worked his way up to the Group ring. It's the "working your way up" part that you must keep in mind.

Assuming that you have

Many owners, on the other hand, enter their "average" Bloodhounds in dog shows for the fun and enjoyment of it. Dog showing makes an absorbing hobby with many rewards for dogs and owners alike. If you're having fun, meeting other people who share your interests and enjoying the overall experience, you likely will catch the "bug." Once the dog-show bug bites, its effects can last a lifetime; it's like a deer tick, but good instead! Soon you will be

Whether you are a novice exhibitor or a seasoned professional, the sport of dog showing offers much excitement and camaraderie.

envisioning yourself in the center ring at the Westminster Kennel Club Dog Show in New York City, competing for the prestigious Best in Show cup. This magical dog show is televised annually from Madison Square Garden, and the victorious dog becomes a celebrity overnight.

AKC CONFORMATION SHOWING

GETTING STARTED
Visiting a dog show as a spectator is a great place to start. Pick up the show catalog to find out what time your breed is being shown, who is judging the breed and in which ring the classes will be held. To start, Bloodhounds compete against other Bloodhounds, and the winner is selected as Best of Breed by the judge. This is the procedure for each breed. At a group show, all of the Best of Breed winners go on to compete for Group One in their respective group. For example, all Best of Breed winners for each breed in the Hound Group compete against each other; this is done for all seven groups. Finally, all seven

CLASSES AT DOG SHOWS

There can be as many as 18 classes per sex for your breed. Check the show schedule carefully to make sure that you have entered your dog in the appropriate class. The classes offered can include Minor Puppy (ages 6 to 9 months), Puppy (ages 6 to 12 months), Junior (ages 6 to 18 months) and Beginners (handler or dog has never won first place), as well as the following, each of which is defined in the schedule: Maiden; Novice; Tyro; Debutant; Undergraduate; Graduate; Post-graduate; Minor Limit; Mid Limit; Limit; Open; Veteran; Stud Dog; Brood Bitch; Progeny; Brace and Team.

group winners go head to head in the ring for the Best in Show award.

What most spectators don't understand is the basic idea of conformation. A dog show is often referred to as a "conformation" show. This means that the judge should decide how each dog stacks up (conforms) to the breed standard for his given breed: how well does this Bloodhound conform to the ideal representative detailed in the standard? Ideally, this is what happens. In reality, however, this ideal often gets slighted as the judge compares Bloodhound #1 to Bloodhound #2. Again, the ideal is that each dog is judged based on his merits in comparison to his breed standard, not in comparison to the other dogs in the ring. It is easier for judges to compare dogs of the same breed to decide which he thinks is the better specimen; in the Group and Best in Show ring, however, it is very difficult to compare one breed to another, like apples to oranges. Thus the dog's conformation to the breed standard—not to mention good handling and advertising—is essential to his success.

The breed standard, which is drafted and approved by the breed's national parent club, the American Bloodhound Club, is then submitted to the American Kennel Club (AKC). The dog described in the standard is the perfect dog of that breed, and breeders keep their eye on the standard when they choose which dogs to breed, hoping to get closer and closer to the ideal with each litter.

Another good first step for the novice is to join a dog club. You will be astonished by the many and different kinds of dog clubs in the country, with about 5,000 clubs holding events every year. Most clubs require that prospective new members present two letters of recommendation from existing members. Perhaps you've made some friends visiting a show held by a particular club and you would like to join that club. Dog clubs may specialize in a single breed, like a local or regional Bloodhound club, or in a specific pursuit, such as obedience, tracking or hunting tests. There are all-breed clubs for all dog enthusiasts, which sponsor special training days, seminars on topics like grooming or handling or lectures on breeding or canine genetics. There are also clubs that specialize in certain types of dogs, like herding dogs, hunting dogs, companion dogs, etc.

A parent club is the national organization, sanctioned by the AKC, which promotes and safeguards its breed in the country. The American Bloodhound Club was formed in 1952 and can be contacted on the Internet at www.bloodhound.org. The parent club holds an annual national

specialty show, usually in a different city each year, in which many of the country's top dogs, handlers and breeders gather to compete. At a specialty show, only members of a single breed are invited to participate. There are also Group specialties, in which all members of a Group are invited. For more information about dog clubs in your area, contact the AKC at www.akc.org on the Internet or write them at their Raleigh, NC address.

Dog shows offer an enjoyable outlet for novices and professionals alike. There's much to learn about the world of showing.

HOW SHOWS ARE ORGANIZED

Three kinds of conformation show are offered by the AKC. There is the all-breed show, in which all

AKC-recognized breeds can compete; the specialty show, which is for one breed only and usually sponsored by the breed's parent club; and the Group show,

SEAL OF EXCELLENCE

The show ring is the testing ground for a breeder's program. A championship on a dog signifies that three qualified judges have placed their seal of approval on him. Only dogs that have earned their championships should be considered for breeding purposes. Striving to improve the breed and reproduce sound, typical examples of the breed, breeders must breed only the best. No breeder only breeds for pet homes; they strive for the top. The goal of every program must be to better the breed, and every responsible breeder wants the prestige of producing Best in Show winners.

for all breeds in one of the seven AKC groups. The Bloodhound competes in the Hound Group.

For a dog to become an AKC champion of record, the dog must earn 15 points at shows. The points must be awarded by at least three different judges and must include two "majors" under different judges. A "major" is a three-, four- or five-point win, and the number of points per win is determined by the number of dogs competing in the show on that day. Dogs that are absent or are excused are not counted. The number of points that are awarded varies from breed to breed. More dogs are needed to attain a major in more popular breeds, and fewer dogs are needed in less popular breeds. Yearly, the AKC evaluates the number of dogs in competition in each division (there are 14 divisions in all, based on geography) and may or may not change the numbers of dogs required for each number of points. For example, a major in Division 2 (Delaware, New Jersey and Pennsylvania) recently required 17 dogs or 16 bitches for a three-point major, 29 dogs or 27 bitches for a four-point major and 51 dogs or 46 bitches for a five-point major. The Bloodhound attracts a fair number of entrants at all-breed shows, not as many as breeds like the Poodle or Labrador Retriever.

Only one dog and one bitch of

each breed can win points at a given show. There are no "co-ed" classes except for champions of record. Dogs and bitches do not compete against each other until they are champions. Dogs that are not champions (referred to as "class dogs") compete in one of five classes. The class in which a dog is entered depends on age and previous show wins. First, there is the Puppy Class (sometimes divided further into classes for 6- to 9-month-olds and 9- to 12-month-olds); next is the Novice Class (for dogs that have no points toward their championship and whose only first-place wins have come in the Puppy Class or the Novice Class, the latter class limited to three first places); then there is the American-bred Class (for dogs bred in the US); the Bred-by-Exhibitor Class (for dogs handled by their breeders or by immediate family members of their breeders) and the Open Class (for any non-champions). Any dog may enter the Open class, regardless of age or win history, but, to be competitive, the dog should be older and have ring experience.

The judge at the show begins judging the dogs in the Puppy Class(es) and proceeds through the other classes. The judge awards first through fourth place in each class. The first-place winners of each class then compete with one another in the Winners Class to determine Winners Dog. The judge

A bitch who excels in the show ring may also be a candidate for a breeding program. Owners with hopes of pursuing a show career with their new charges should seek out the puppies of Bloodhounds who have won titles in the show ring.

then starts over with the bitches, beginning with the Puppy Class(es) and proceeding up to the Winners Class to award Winners Bitch, just as he did with the dogs. A Reserve Winners Dog and Reserve Winners Bitch are also selected; these could be awarded the points in the case of a disqualification.

The Winners Dog and Winners Bitch are the two that are awarded the points for their breed. They then go on to compete with any champions of record (often called "specials") of their breed that are entered in the show. The champions may be dogs or bitches; in this class, all are shown together. The judge reviews the Winners Dog and Winners Bitch along with all of the champions to select the Best of Breed winner. The Best of Winners is selected between the Winners Dog and Winners Bitch; if one of these two is selected Best of Breed as well, he or she is automatically determined Best of Winners. Lastly, the judge selects Best of Opposite Sex to the Best of Breed winner. The Best of Breed winner then goes on to the Group competition.

At a Group or all-breed show, the Best of Breed winners from each breed are divided into their respective groups to compete against one another for Group One through Group Four. Group One (first place) is awarded to the dog that best lives up to the ideal for his breed as described in the standard. A Group judge, therefore, must have a thorough working knowledge of many breed standards. After placements have been made in each Group, the seven Group One winners (from the Sporting Group, Toy Group, Hound Group, etc.) compete against each other for the top honor, Best in Show.

There are different ways to find out about dog shows in your area. The American Kennel Club's monthly magazine, the *American Kennel Gazette* is accompanied by the *Events Calendar*; this magazine is available through subscription. You can also look on the AKC's and your parent club's websites for information, and check the event listings in your local newspaper.

Your Bloodhound must be six months of age or older and registered with the AKC in order to be entered in AKC-sanctioned shows in which there are classes for the Bloodhound. Your Bloodhound also must not possess any disqualifying faults and must be sexually intact. The reason for the latter is simple: dog shows are the proving grounds to determine which dogs and bitches are worthy of being bred. If they cannot be bred, that defeats the purpose! On that note, only dogs that have achieved championships, thus proving their excellent quality, should be bred. If you have spayed or neutered your dog, you can participate in tracking trials and the Canine Good Citizen® program.

FOLLOW YOUR NOSE

Although there are a number of organized competitions available to owners of pure-bred dogs, Bloodhounds are not ideally suited to most of these. Working trials, agility trials, obedience shows, field trials, etc., are designed to test dogs' abilities, all requiring much specialized training and considerable financial and time investments. Beyond man-trailing events, the Bloodhound's life revolves around his master and family and community-oriented service skills like search and rescue, PAT therapy-dog work, detection work, etc.

In the US, Bloodhounds excel at tracking trials, based on the same principles as man-trailing, the dog's natural ability to follow human scent. These trials, endorsed by the American Kennel

Club, give the dog the opportunity to add tracking suffixes to their names.

The first AKC-licensed tracking test took place in 1937 as part of the Utility level at an obedience trial, and thus competitive tracking was officially begun. The first title, Tracking Dog (TD), was offered in 1947, ten years after the first official tracking test. It was not until 1980 that the AKC added the title Tracking Dog Excellent (TDX), which was followed by the title Versatile Surface Tracking (VST) in 1995. Champion Tracker (CT) is awarded to a dog who has earned all three of these titles.

The TD level is the first and most basic level in tracking, progressing in difficulty to the TDX and then the VST. A dog must follow a track laid by a human 30 to 120 minutes prior in order to earn the TD title. The track is about 500 yards long and contains up to 5 directional changes. At the next level, the TDX, the dog must follow a 3- to 5-hour-old track over a course that is up to 1,000 yards long and has up to 7 directional changes. In the most difficult level, the VST, the track is up to 5 hours old and located in an urban setting.

All of these titles are awarded based on the dog's performance, demonstrating that the dog can locate an article that has been dropped by a track layer minutes or hours previously. The more difficult trials cover greater

Awaiting her turn in the show ring, this Bloodhound sits in the benching area at a large all-breed show. Bench shows are ideal for visitors to meet the breeders and the dogs when they are not busy with the competition.

distances of time and space, possibly dropping a leather glove miles away three or four days prior on a less direct course with various scenting obstacles. The VST is awarded to a dog that demonstrates his ability to follow a track in an urban setting to simulate a real tracking situation. There are tracking clubs that can be contacted for more information, and these can be reached through the AKC.

You chose your dog because something clicked the minute you set eyes on him. Or perhaps it seemed that the dog selected you and that's what clinched the deal. Either way, you are now investing time and money in this dog, a true pal and an outstanding member of the family. Everything about him is perfect—well, almost perfect. Remember, he is a dog. For that matter, how does he think you're doing?

UNDERSTANDING THE CANINE MINDSET

For starters, you and your dog are on different wavelengths. Your dog is similar to a toddler in that both live in the present tense only. A dog's view of life is based primarily on cause and effect, which is similar to the old saying, "Nothing teaches a youngster to hang on like falling off the swing." If your dog stumbles down a flight of three steps, the next time he will try the Superman approach and fling himself off the top one!

Your dog makes connections based on the fact that he lives in the present, so when he is doing something and you interrupt to dispense praise or a correction, a connection, positive or negative, is made. To the dog, that's like one plus one equals two! In the same sense, it's also easy to see that when your timing is off, you will cause an incorrect connection. The one-plus-one way of thinking is why you must never scold a dog for behavior that took place an hour, 15 minutes or even 15 seconds ago. But it is also why, when your timing is perfect, you can teach him to do all kinds of wonderful things—as soon as he has made that essential connection. What helps the process is his desire to please you and to have your approval.

There are behaviors we admire in dogs, such as friendliness and obedience, as well as those behaviors that cause problems to a varying degree. The dog owner who encounters minor behavior problems is wise to solve them promptly or get professional help. Bad behaviors are not corrected by repeatedly shouting "No" or getting angry with the dog. Only praise and approval for good behavior lets your dog understand right from wrong. The longer a bad behavior is allowed to continue, the harder it is to overcome. A responsible breeder is often able to help. Each dog is unique, even within a specific breed, so try not to compare your dog's behavior with your neighbor's dog or the one you had as a child.

Have your veterinarian check the dog to see if a behavior problem could have a physical cause. An earache or toothache, for example, could be the reason for a dog to snap at you if you were to touch his head when putting on his leash. A sharp correction from you would only increase the behavior. When a physical basis is eliminated, and if the problem is not something you understand or can cope with, ask for the name of a behavioral specialist, preferably one who is familiar with your breed. Be sure to keep the breeder informed of your progress.

Many things, such as environment and inherited traits, form the basic behavior of a dog, just as in humans. You also must factor into his temperament the purpose for which your dog was originally bred. The major obstacle lies in the dog's inability to explain his behavior to us in a way that we understand. The one thing you should not do is to give up and abandon your dog. Somewhere a misunderstanding has occurred but, with help and patient understanding on your part, you should be able to work out the majority of bothersome behaviors.

EXIT STAGE LEFT

Your dog studies your every move. He knows that before you leave the house, you gather a bunch of stuff, put on your coat and shake your keys. His anxiety emerges at the first sight of seeing you begin your "exit routine." If your dog suffers from separation anxiety, you should rethink your exit. Mix up your routine and include your dog in some of the tasks. Play a short game of fetch, reward the dog for a couple of commands, present him with a fun, safe toy and give him a treat before you leave the house. If the dog is exercised, content and focused on something other than your exit, he may learn to adapt better to your absence.

SEPARATION ANXIETY

Any behaviorist will tell you that separation anxiety is the most common problem about which pet owners complain. It is also one of the easiest to prevent, or even to solve. Unfortunately, a behaviorist usually is not consulted until the dog is a stressed-out, neurotic mess. At that stage, it is indeed a problem that requires the help of a professional.

Training the puppy to the fact that people in the house come and go is essential in order to avoid this anxiety. Leaving the puppy in his crate or a confined area while family members go in and out, and stay out for longer and longer periods of time, is the basic way to desensitize the pup to the family's frequent departures. If you are at home most of every day, make it a point to go out for at least an hour or two whenever possible.

How you leave is vital to the dog's reaction. Your dog is no fool. He knows the difference between sweats and business suits, jeans and dresses. He sees you pat your pocket to check for your wallet, open your briefcase, check that you have your cell phone or pick up the car keys. He knows from the hurry of the kids in the morning that they're off to school until afternoon. Lipstick? Aftershave lotion? Lunch boxes? Every move you make registers in

I GOTTA RIGHT TO SING THE BLUES

The term "separation anxiety" resonates with modern-day "psychobabble" overtones and, therefore, may be shunned by dog owners as an imaginary New Age disorder. On the contrary, veterinary behaviorists have begun to treat the condition like a real problem. Recently some drug therapies that have shown positive effects on dogs who suffer from separation anxiety have entered the market; among the most successful are Prozac and Clomicalm.

If anti-anxiety drugs don't work, consider getting your canine pal a pal of his own. Introducing a second dog to the household may do wonders for your dog's spirits. For dog owners who must be out of the house for eight hours or more hours a day for work, a second dog is an excellent choice. Another option is to hire a dog walker or dog sitter so that your dog isn't alone for long periods of time. There are also doggie day-care centers that offer reliable services at reasonable prices. Check your phone book for listings or take a look online for facilities in your area. More and more dog owners use their services, so ask around to get recommendations.

his sensory perception and memory. Your puppy knows more about your departure than the CIA or the FBI. You can't get away with a thing!

Some Bloodhounds will go to great lengths to communicate with their human masters.

An adult Bloodhound jumping up can be dangerous to everyone. Train your puppy *never* to jump up on people.

Before you got dressed, you checked the dog's water bowl and his supply of toys (including a long-lasting chew toy), and turned the radio on low. You will leave him in what he considers his "safe" area, not with total freedom of the house. If you've invested in child safety gates, you can be reasonably sure that he'll remain in the designated area. Don't give him access to a window where he can watch you leave the house. If you're leaving for an hour or two, just put him in his crate with a safe toy.

Now comes the test! You are ready to walk out the door. Do not give your dog a big hug and a fond farewell. Do not drag out a long goodbye. Those are the very things that jump-start separation anxiety. Toss a biscuit into the dog's area, call out "So long, pooch" and close the door. You're

gone. The chances are that the dog may bark a couple of times, or maybe whine once or twice, and then settle down to enjoy his biscuit and take a lovely nap, especially if you took him for a nice long walk after breakfast. As he grows up, the barks and whines will stop because it's an old routine, so why should he make the effort?

When you first brought home the puppy, the come-and-go routine was intermittent and constant. He was put in his crate with a tiny treat. You left (silently) and returned in 3 minutes, then 5, then 10, then15, then half an hour, until finally you could leave without a problem and be gone for two or three hours. If, at any time in the future, there's a "separation" problem, refresh his memory by going back to that basic training.

Now comes the next most important part—your return. Do not make a big production of coming home. "Hi, poochie" is as grand a greeting as he needs. When you've taken off your hat and coat, tossed your briefcase on the hall table and glanced at the mail, and the dog has settled down from the excitement of seeing you "in person" from his confined area, then go and give him a warm, friendly greeting. A potty trip is needed and a walk would be appreciated, since he's been such a good dog.

BARKING

Blessed with a big hound voice, the Bloodhound has a knack for expressing himself vocally. Barking is a dog's way of "talking." It can be somewhat frustrating because it is not always easy to tell what a dog means by his bark—is he excited, happy, frightened or angry? Whatever it is that the dog is trying to say, he should not be punished for barking. It is only when the barking becomes excessive, and when the excessive barking becomes a bad habit, that the behavior needs to be modified.

Bloodhounds tend to be vocal when outdoors, especially when they are on a trail or have located their quarry. They have a resonant, melodious voice, a cross between baying and a sing-song howl.

Here's a big, noisy problem! Telling a dog he must never bark is like telling a child not to speak! Consider how confusing it must be to your dog that you are using your voice (which is your form of barking) to teach him when to bark and when not to! That is precisely the reason not to "bark back" when the dog's barking is annoying you (or your neighbors). Try to understand the scenario from the dog's viewpoint. He barks. You bark. He barks again, you bark again. This "conversation"can go on forever!

The first time your adorable little puppy said "Yip" or "Yap," you were ecstatic. His first word! You smiled, you told him how smart he was—and you allowed him to do it. So there's that one-plus-one thing again, because he will understand by your happy reaction, "Mr. Alpha loves it when I talk." Ignore his barking in the beginning, and allow it, but don't encourage barking during play. Instead, use the "put a toy in it" method to tone it down. Add a very soft "Quiet" as you hand off

QUIET DOWN!

If your dog barks excessively, don't bark back. Yelling at him only encourages him to keep it up. Barking at the garbage truck makes perfect sense to the dog—that man is stealing your garbage! When the garbage truck leaves, that spells success to the dog: he has scared away the garbage man with his bark! Pick a command word, something like "Quiet" or "No Bark," to stop his barking. The second he stops, tell him "Good dog" and toss him a toy.

LOOK AT ME WHEN I SPEAK TO YOU

Your dog considers direct eye contact as a sign of dominance. A shy dog will avoid looking at you; a dominant dog will try to stare you down. What you want is for your dog to pay attention when you speak, and that doesn't necessarily involve direct eye contact. In dealing with a problem dog, avert your gaze momentarily, return to face the dog and give an immediate down command. Show him that you are the boss.

the toy. If the barking continues, stand up straight, fold your arms and turn your back on the dog. If he barks, you won't play, and you should follow the same rule for all undesirable behavior during play.

Dogs bark in reaction to sounds and sights. Another dog's bark, a person passing by or even just rustling leaves can set off a barker. If someone coming up your driveway or to your door provokes a barking frenzy, use the saturation method to stop it. Have several friends come and go every three or four minutes over as long a period of time as they can spare (it could take a couple of hours). Attach about a foot of rope to the dog's collar and have very small treats handy. Each time a car pulls up or a person approaches, let the

dog bark once (grab the rope if you need to physically restrain him), say "Okay, good dog," give him a treat and make him sit. "Okay" is the release command. It lets the dog know that he has alerted you and tells him that you are now in charge. That person leaves and the next arrives, and so on and so on until everyone— especially the dog—is bored and the barking has stopped. Don't forget to thank your friends. Your neighbors, by the way, may be more than willing to assist you in this parlor game.

Excessive barking outdoors is more difficult to keep in check because, when it happens, he is outside and you are probably inside. A few warning barks are fine, but use the same method to tell him when enough is enough. You will have to stay outside with him for that bit of training.

There is one more kind of vocalizing which is called "idiot barking" (from idiopathic or of unknown cause). It is usually rhythmic or a timed series of barks. Put a stop to it immediately by calling the dog to come. This form of barking can drive neighbors crazy and commonly occurs when a dog is left outside at night or for long periods of time during the day. He is completely and thoroughly bored! A change of scenery may help, such as relocating him to a room indoors when he is used to being outside. A few new toys or different dog biscuits might be the solution. If he is left alone and no one can get home during the day, a noontime walk with a local dog-sitter would be the perfect solution.

AGGRESSION

"Aggression" is a word that is often misunderstood and is sometimes even used to describe what is actually normal canine behavior. For example, it's normal for puppies to growl when playing tug-of-war. It's puppy talk. There are different forms of dog aggression, but all are degrees of dominance, indicating that the dog, not his master, is (or thinks he is) in control. When the dog feels that he (or his control of the situation) is threatened, he will respond. The extent of the aggressive behavior varies with individual dogs. It is not at all pleasant to see bared teeth or to hear your dog growl or snarl, but these are signs of behavior that, if left uncorrected, can become extremely dangerous. A word of warning here: never challenge an aggressive dog. He is unpredictable and therefore unreliable to approach.

Nothing gets a "hello" from strangers on the street quicker than walking a puppy, but people should ask permission before petting your dog so you can tell him to sit in order to receive the admiring pats. If a hand comes down over the dog's head and he shrinks back, ask the person to bring their hand up, underneath the pup's chin. Now you're correcting strangers, too! But, if you don't, it could make your dog afraid of strangers, which in turn can lead to fear-biting. Socialization prevents much of aggression before it rears its ugly head.

The body language of an aggressive dog about to attack is clear. The dog will have a hard, steady stare. He will try to look as big as possible by standing stiff-legged, pushing out his chest, keeping his ears up and holding his tail up and steady. The hackles on his back will rise so that a ridge of hairs stands up. This posture may include the

LEAD THE WAY

A dog that's becoming unreliable in his behavior needs to have his trust in your leadership reinforced. Are you being consistent, patient and fair? Consistent means that you are using the same words to expect the same response every time. Patient means that you haven't made the task clearly enough for your dog to understand, so you must persevere until you get the message across. Fair means that you see things from the dog's point of view. Angry words or physical punishment are unacceptable from a trusted leader.

curled lip, snarl and/or growl, or
he may be silent. He looks, and
definitely is, very dangerous.

This dominant posture is seen
in dogs that are territorially
aggressive. Deliverymen are
constant victims of serious bites
from such dogs. Territorial aggression is the reason you should
never, ever, try to train a puppy to
be a watchdog. It can escalate into
the type of behavior over which
you will have no control. All
forms of aggression must be taken
seriously and dealt with immediately. If signs of aggressive
behavior continue, or grow worse,
or if you are at all unsure about
how to deal with your dog's
behavior, get the help of a professional.

MATTERS OF SEX
For whatever reasons, real or
imagined, most people tend to
have a preference in choosing
between a male or female puppy.
Some, but not all of the undesirable traits attributed to the sex of
the dog can be suppressed by
early spaying or neutering. The
major advantage, of course, is that
a neutered male or a spayed
female will not be adding to the
overpopulation of dogs.

An unaltered male will mark
territory by lifting his leg
everywhere, leaving a few drops
of urine indoors on your furniture
and appliances, and outside on
everything he passes. It is difficult

PROFESSIONAL HELP
Every trainer and behaviorist asks,
"Why didn't you come to me
sooner?" Pet owners often don't
want to admit that anything is wrong
with their dogs. A dog's problem
often is due to the dog and his owner
mixing their messages, which will
only get worse. Don't put it off;
consult a professional to find out
whether or not the problem is
serious enough to require
intervention.

to catch him in the act, because
he only leaves a few drops each
time, but it is very hard to
eliminate the odor. Thus the cycle
begins, because the odor will
entice him to mark that spot
again.

If you have bought a bitch
with the intention of breeding her,
be sure you know what you are
getting into. She will go through
one or two periods of estrus each
year, each cycle lasting about
three weeks. During these times,
she will have to be kept confined
to protect your furniture and to
protect her from being bred by a
male other than the one you have
selected. Breeding should never
be undertaken to "show the kids
the miracle of birth." Bitches can
die giving birth, and the puppies
may also die. The dam often
exhibits what is called "maternal
aggression" after the pups are

born. Her intention is to protect her pups, but in fact she can be extremely vicious. Breeding should be left to the experienced breeders, who do so for the betterment of the breed and with much research and planning behind each mating.

Mounting is not unusual in dogs, male or female. Puppies do it to each other and adults do it regardless of sex, because it is not so much a sexual act as it is one of dominance. It becomes very annoying when the dog mounts your legs, the kids or the couch cushions; in these and other instances of mounting, he should be corrected. Touching sometimes stimulates the dog, so pulling the dog off by his collar or leash, together with a consistent and stern "Off!" command, usually eliminates the behavior.

CHEWING

All puppies chew. All dogs chew. This is a fact of life for canines, and sometimes you may think it's what your dog does best! A pup starts chewing when his first set of teeth erupt and continues throughout the teething period. Chewing gives the pup relief from itchy gums and incoming teeth and, from that time on, he gets great satisfaction out of this normal, somewhat idle, canine activity. Providing safe chew toys is the best way to direct this behavior in an appropriate

manner. Chew toys are available in all sizes, textures and flavors, but you must monitor the wear-and-tear inflicted on your pup's toys to be sure that the ones you've chosen are safe and remain in good condition.

Puppies cannot distinguish between a rawhide toy and a nice leather shoe or wallet. It's up to you to keep your possessions away from the dog and to keep your eye on the dog. There's a form of destruction caused by chewing that is not the dog's fault. Let's say you allow him on the sofa. One day he takes a rawhide bone up on the sofa and, in the course of chewing on the bone, takes up a bit of fabric. He continues to chew. Disaster! Now you've learned the lesson: dogs with chew toys have to be either kept off furniture and carpets, carefully supervised or put in their confined areas for chew time.

Have an array of safe chews on hand for your Bloodhound. Wouldn't you rather offer him something to chew rather than leaving him to his own devices?

The wooden legs of furniture are favorite objects for chewing. The first time, tell the dog "Leave it!" (or "No!") and offer him a chew toy as a substitute. But your clever dog may be hiding under the chair and doing some silent destruction, which you may not notice until it's too late. In this case, it's time to try one of the foul-tasting products, made specifically to prevent destructive chewing, that can be sprayed on the objects of your dog's chewing attention. These products also work to keep the dog away from plants, trash, etc. It's even a good way to stop the dog from "mouthing" or chewing on your hands or the leg of your pants. (Be sure to wash your hands after the mouthing lesson!) A little spray goes a long way.

DIGGING

Digging is another natural, normal, doggy behavior. Wild canines dig to bury whatever food they can save for later to eat. (And you thought we invented the doggy bag!) Burying bones or toys is a primary reason to dig. Dogs also dig to get at interesting little underground creatures like moles and mice. In the summer, they dig to get down to cool earth. In winter, they dig to get beneath the cold surface to warmer earth.

The solution to the last two is easy. In the summer, provide a bed that's up off the ground and placed in a shaded area. In winter, the dog should either be indoors to sleep or given an adequate insulated doghouse outdoors. To understand how natural and normal this is you have only to consider the Nordic breeds of sled dog who, at the end of the run, routinely dig a bed for themselves in the snow. It's the nesting instinct. How often have you seen your dog go round and round in circles, pawing at his blanket or bedding before flopping down to sleep?

Domesticated dogs also dig to escape, and that's a lot more dangerous than it is destructive. A dog that digs under the fence is the one that is hit by a car or becomes lost. A good fence to protect a digger should be set 10 to 12 inches below ground level, and every fence needs to be routinely checked for even the smallest openings that can become possible escape routes.

Catching your dog in the act of digging is the easiest way to stop it, because your dog will make the "one-plus-one" connection, but digging is too often a solitary occupation, something the lonely dog does out of boredom. Catch your young puppy in the act and put a stop to it before you have a yard full of craters. It is more difficult to stop if your dog sees you gardening. If you can dig, why can't he? Because you say so, that's why!

STOP, THIEF!

The easiest way to prevent a dog from stealing food is to stop this behavior before it starts by never leaving food out where he can reach it. However, if it is too late, and your dog has already made a steal, you must stop your furry felon from becoming a repeat offender. Once Sneaky Pete has successfully stolen food, place a bit of food where he can reach it. Place an empty soda can with some pebbles in it on top of the food. Leave the room and watch what happens. As the dog grabs the tasty morsel, the can comes with it. The noise of the tumbling pebble-filled can makes its own correction, and you don't have to say a word.

Some breeds are excavation experts, and some dogs never dig. However, when it comes to any of these instinctive canine behaviors, never say "never."

FOOD-RELATED PROBLEMS

We're not talking about eating, diets or nutrition here, we're talking about bad habits. Face it. All dogs are beggars. Food is the motivation for everything we want our dogs to do and, when you combine that with their innate ability to "con" us in order to get their way, it's a wonder there aren't far more obese dogs in the world.

Who can resist the bleeding-heart look that says "I'm starving," or the paw that gently pats your knee and gives you a knowing look, or the whining "please" or even the total body language of a perfect sit beneath the cookie jar. No one who professes to love his dog can turn down the pleas of his clever canine's performances every time. One thing is for sure, though: definitely do not allow begging at the table. Family meals do not include your dog.

Control your dog's begging habit by making him work for his rewards. Ignore his begging when you can. Utilize the obedience commands you've taught your dog. Use "Off" for the pawing. A sit or even a long down will interrupt the whining. His reward in these situations is definitely not a treat! Casual verbal praise is enough. Be sure all members of the family follow the same rules.There is a different type of begging that does demand your immediate response and that is the appeal to be let (or taken) outside! Usually that is a quick paw or small whine to get your attention, followed by a race to the door. This type of begging needs your quick attention and approval. Of course, a really smart dog will soon figure out how to cut you off at the pass and direct you to that cookie jar on your way to the door! Some dogs are always one step ahead of us.

INDEX

My Bloodhound

PUT YOUR PUPPY'S FIRST PICTURE HERE

Dog's Name _____

Date _____ Photographer _____